P9-BZS-635

The
100 Best
VEGAN
BAKING
Recipes

The 100 Best  BAKING Recipes

Amazing
Cookies, Cakes,
Muffins, Pies,
Brownies and
Breads

Kris Holechek

Ulysses Press

Copyright text © 2009 by Kris Holechek. Copyright design © 2009 Ulysses Press and its licensors. All Rights Reserved. Any unauthorized duplication in whole or in part or dissemination of this edition by any means (including but not limited to photocopying, electronic bulletin boards, and the Internet) will be prosecuted to the fullest extent of the law.

Published by Ulysses Press
    P.O. Box 3440
    Berkeley, CA 94703
    www.ulyssespress.com

ISBN: 978-1-56975-714-7
Library of Congress Catalog Number 2009902006

Printed in the United States by Bang Printing

10 9 8 7 6 5

Acquisitions Editor: Nick Denton-Brown
Managing Editor: Claire Chun
Editors: Lauren Harrison, Elyce Pekter
Proofreader: Kate Kellogg
Production: Judith Metzener, Abigail Reser
Cover design: DiAnna Van Eycke
Cover photos: cupcake © Hannah Kaminsky/www.bittersweetblog.blogpress.com; cookie
    © Shaun Lowe Photographic/www.istockphoto.com; bundt cake © Carmen Steiner/
    www.shutterstock.com; brownie © Kathy Burns-Millyard/www.shutterstock.com
Interior design: what!design @ whatweb.com

This book is sold for information purposes only. Neither the author nor the publisher will be held accountable for the use or misuse of the information contained in this book. This book is not intended as medical advice, because the author and publisher of this work are not medical doctors and do not recommend the use of medicines to achieve relief from ailments associated with sugar and wheat. The author, publisher, and distributor of this book are not responsible for any adverse effects or consequences resulting from the use of any recipes, suggestions, or procedures described hereafter.

To Dad, for teaching me to want more, follow my heart and make it happen
and
To Jim, fabulous husband and best friend: You doin' it right.

TABLE OF CONTENTS

PREFACE

I was raised in an unconventional home, mostly around my grandparents. My mother's ideas of cooking and baking ended somewhere between the microwave door and premade cookie dough. But my grandmothers—wow, could they bake! I quickly became a baking addict. I didn't wait up on Christmas Eve to sneak a peek at Santa; I waited until the adults went to bed to raid my grandmother's Christmas cookie reserves. Providing delicious food, in the good times and the bad, was how my grandmothers showed their love. Even when times are tough, it doesn't require much to whip together some cookies or a cake, and the joy that it can bring is priceless.

Baking was something I rarely had the chance to do in my parents' house growing up, so it was reserved for special occasions at my aunt's house or trips to see my grandmothers. Once I moved into my own place, my kitchen was never clean again and I'm all the fatter, I mean, better for it! My favorite thing to provide my family and friends is a warm meal and a row of desserts.

When I became vegan, I was driven by the ethics of it, and I went into it with the assumption that the flavors I had grown to love were going to disappear and life would be bland, especially when it came to baking. My mind was filled with visions of oat bran and whole-wheat flour, unappetizing brown blobs that no one would be eager to eat. I couldn't have been more wrong! My husband, Jim, and I always talk about how the food we eat as vegans is much more flavorful and satisfying than the food we ate when we were still courting cow's milk and eggs.

Vegan baking was the first thing I jumped into when we made the change, and I was delighted to find that everything I enjoyed in my egg-eating days was still delicious and, in many cases, even better! Soon, I was in baking overdrive, concocting new creations and adapting old favorites. As cakes, cookies and breads started taking over our house, Jim suggested that I write a book. That book, *The Damn Tasty Vegan Baking Guide*, came out in May of 2007. A year and half later I was invited to compile a new book, which would include my previous recipes, along with a complete update. This expanded the book to over twice the size! The challenge of creating a whole new batch of recipes got the creative juices flowing and soon our house once again turned into a patisserie.

Baking is magical and mysterious. You mix up some basic ingredients, create a moist, sticky substance and it turns into a treat that could pacify the world's biggest cranky pants. Once it is in the oven, it's out of bounds, which can prove scary to some people, especially those who fancy cooking. My primary goal with this book (aside from providing vegan treats that taste great!) is to offer tips and tricks that can shed light on some new methods, to demystify how baking works and to help inspire you to pick up a spatula and make a wowzer of a cake. My other objective is to make this book as approachable as possible. Whether you are a first-time baker or a seasoned flour-slinger, you will find recipes to fit your skill level. Don't be afraid to try something challenging, just be sure to read all of the instructions before starting so there are no surprises. I also made a point to make the ingredients as easy to come by as possible. There are a lot of exotic ingredients that can be fun to bake with, but they aren't necessary. You don't need to run to two co-ops and an Asian grocery store to gather the ingredients for a pie. I tried to keep the ingredients as big-box-grocer-friendly as possible to make your baking prep easy. In addition to this book, there is a whole website devoted to my recipes, complete with pictures of the goodies, tutorials, tips and my blog. Please stop by www.nomnomnomblog.com and check it out!

Baking is my gift to my family. I hope you enjoy these recipes enough to give them to your loved ones, as well. From picky eaters to food snobs, everyone will appreciate these recipes and they'll never know it's vegan!

Happy Baking,
Kris

ACKNOWLEDGMENTS

This book was delightful to make and there are many people who had a hand in it. Thank you to my amazing best friend and partner in crime, Jim, for all your taste-testing, grocery store runs and entertainment. Thank you to all of the friends who recipe-tested, recipe-tasted and otherwise put up with me: Amy, Sandy and Leslie, you are all wonderful. Thank you to my wonderful grandmothers for instilling in me such a passion for baking that a day doesn't go by where I don't dream of my next pastry. Thank you, of course, to my family for always being there. Thank you to all of my wonderful blog readers for your support and community. Thank you to the kind folks at Ulysses Press for having such good taste in books. Last, but certainly not least, thank you to my father, Randy, for always believing in me, encouraging my dreams no matter how far-fetched they seemed and for teaching me what a real work ethic is. I wish you could see this.

VEGAN BAKING: AN INTRODUCTION

Vegan baking means using no animal products. No eggs, no milk or cream, no butter and, for some people, no honey. This also means products that contain these things are out, like commercially made frosting or Cool Whip.

Vegan baking may seem impossible, especially if you are someone who has been subjected to some awful vegan baked goods. But it's not veganism that makes them bad. Think of how many conventional baked goods you have had that were lackluster or downright gross. Dry, crumbly cakes, hard cookies, soggy pies—we've all eaten them. And let's be honest...the first time you ate a vegan baked good, didn't you expect something to taste different, and so it did? A delicious vegan baked good is not about what's in it (or what's not, for that matter), it's about technique and having a well-written recipe to work from.

Baking without animal products may seem like a radical concept, but it's truly not. There are plenty of foods out there that are naturally vegan and no one is the wiser; the recipes are just that good. During WWII when many goods were rationed, women in the U.S. became revolutionary bakers, swapping out animal products for things as far-reaching as salad dressing to continue making baked goods. Vegan baking isn't limited to times of hardship. Many cookbooks, restaurants and companies all have prized recipes that are coincidentally vegan. So I'm not advocating the use of Italian dressing in a cake, because wacky things like that aren't necessary. You can easily cut out the animal products and still have cake that is moist and fluffy, cookies that are soft and chewy, and bread that has a texture and flavor you will savor. But vegan baking is more than just eschewing animal ingredients; it's about understanding what role those ingredients play in the recipe and creating the same structure in a cruelty-free way!

I know baking can be very intimidating to some people. Once you put it in the oven it's hands-off, which can be very scary. Let's break things down to get a better understanding of the components of baking. Having this information under our belts will give us the knowledge we need to kick some serious butt in the kitchen!

A COMMON MISCONCEPTION   People often think that vegan baking is inherently healthy. To be clear: It certainly can be, but this book is standard melt-in-your-mouth, creamy, yeasty, frosting-topped fare. This is not health food, and while it would be delicious and quite popular, a diet of vegan baked goods is not advisable.

Vegan baking is, however, cholesterol-free because it is animal-free. Why is it cholesterol-free? Well, cholesterol is created by the liver, so when you consume food that has cholesterol in it, it had to come from someone else's liver. This little factoid makes vegan label-reading a little easier: Anything with cholesterol in it is not vegan. You can do an insta-check to see if a product contains cholesterol and if it does, it saves you time deciphering the list of ingredients.

But, cholesterol aside, vegan baking is just as fatty and sugary as conventional baking—which is what makes it taste so good, even without the eggs and milk!

Before Pancake Batter Came in a Bottle, There Was Flour

Flour is obviously the base for almost all baked goods. There are many kinds of flour, but wheat flour is the standard used in baking. The most common kind is called all-purpose flour, or white flour, which is what is primarily used in this book. White flour is made by stripping away the germ and bran from wheat kernels. This creates the soft, fluffy flour people are most familiar with. This process also strips out much of the wheat's nutritional value, and because we live in a carbohydrate-heavy culture, all-purpose flour is enriched with the nutrients it has lost. Before enriching was a standard practice, some people experienced illnesses related to nutrient-deficiency. During WWII, enriching became standardized in the U.S. and England to help nourish rationed citizens, and it's stuck ever since. All-purpose flour is normally bleached for the sole purpose of making it look whiter. But there is no real visible difference between bleached and unbleached all-purpose flour, and it's just going to get baked, right? Plus, I like to keep my chemical consumption down to a minimum. Thankfully, unbleached all-purpose flour is widely available.

Most grain flours have gluten in them. Gluten is protein, which creates fibers that hold the baked goods together. Some people are allergic to or intolerant of gluten. Because gluten does what it does for baked goods, trying to bake gluten-free can be a challenge. All-purpose flour has a blend of gluten in it that is considered appropriate for, well, all purposes. There are also specific cake and pastry flours that have lower gluten content for lighter baked goods, and higher-gluten flours are also available for bread doughs. These different flours can be fun to play with, but aren't necessary for any of the recipes in this book.

Besides basic white all-purpose flour, there are many other kinds of wheat flour. For regular baking I often use whole-wheat pastry flour, which is made with less processing so there is still some germ and wheat kernel present in the flour. Another great alternative to all-purpose flour is white whole-wheat flour, which is made from a soft white wheat. It has a softer texture than traditional whole-wheat flour, so you can substitute it in your baking without it being very noticeable.

Our love of wheat flour is quite obvious, but there are many other kinds of flour out there. Spelt is a delicious grain that is a descendant of wheat. It has less gluten than wheat flour, but is not gluten-free. Baked goods made with spelt will often be slightly denser than those made with wheat, but it is a very delicious, slightly nutty grain. When substituting spelt flour for wheat flour, you will need to add an additional 2 tablespoons of flour for each cup of wheat flour the recipe calls for.

I also like to use oat flour. You can buy ground oat flour, or just put some traditional dried oats (not steel-cut) into a food processor and blend until it becomes a course flour. Oat flour is not entirely gluten-free, but is very low in gluten. Oat flour adds a pleasant texture to baked goods, as well as extra fiber and protein. Unlike spelt flour, you cannot completely substitute wheat flour with oat flour when baking because of its low gluten content. Oat flour works best when blended with another flour, like all-purpose.

You might also see self-rising flour at grocery stores. This is basic white flour with chemical agents for leavening already added to it. We will talk about leavening later. I prefer to use regular all-purpose and add my own leavening.

There are endless kinds of flour to bake with. From grains to ground-up beans and legumes, you could use a different flour every day for a month and there would still be more to try. This is just an introduction, but I encourage you to do some research and try blending other flours together, such as buckwheat, rice or garbanzo flour. There are too many textures and flavors in the world to limit yourself to just wheat.

Some of the recipes in this book call for flour to be sifted. To sift flour, you put it in a flour sifter, which looks like a metal canister with a handle and usually a crank. There is a mesh bottom to the canister and your crank the flour through it, breaking up any clumps and incorporating air into the flour. Sifters are incredibly easy to come by and are very inexpensive. Recipes that require flour to be sifted are noted.

Binders, Emulsifiers and the Mysterious Inclusion of Eggs

It's easy to read an omnivorous recipe (meaning a recipe for veggie and meat eaters) and feel odd about replacing the eggs. It can feel as if your baked good is disguised as a cake, but is not quite a real cake. And it's certainly easy to let other people make you feel like your cake isn't really a cake, either. So let's explore the function of eggs in baking and look at some other options that will make sure your cake is as real as they come.

Within a baked good, there are certain elements you'll almost always have: a dry base, something to leaven it (make it rise), some sort of fat and something to bind it. In traditional baked goods, the binder is usually an egg. The binder, or emulsifier, acts as a substance that helps hold the baked good. It provides structure, retains moisture, provides a little leavening and helps determine the crumb (texture) of an item. It also helps give the baked good a shelf life. That's a lot of responsibility for one element to achieve. So why eggs? I have no idea. Who saw an egg and thought, "Wow, this will make my cake taste great"? While I'm not sure how eggs became a baking staple, I will tell you that those folks really stopped short of a world of effective, delicious and cholesterol-free options.

There are many binding options to explore. Once you start playing around and reaping the rewards of your experimentation you will realize that these aren't egg replacers, because the eggs never belonged there in the first place! There are so many different textures in baking, you will also see how having more options, rather than using a

MIX AND MATCH

So you have this kick-ass cookbook with over 100 delicious vegan baking recipes in it, but you know what? Eventually, you'll work through the recipes and start dreaming of something different.

I have good news! You have, in your hands, the ability to create endless amounts of treats using a little creativity. In many recipes, I've given you ideas to get you started: Boston Cream Pie can be Banana Cream Pie, or with a little blue food coloring Red Velvet Cupcakes can become Velvet Elvis Cupcakes. There are so many incredible recipes in this book that you can mix and match, giving you limitless possibilities.

default ingredient, can really fine-tune a recipe. Here is a breakdown of some common egg replacers and how to use them:

EGG REPLACER	EQUIVALENT TO 1 EGG	WORKS BEST IN...
Unsweetened applesauce	¼ cup	Cakes, bars, quick breads, muffins and cookies
Plain or vanilla soy yogurt	¼ cup	Cakes, bars, quick breads and muffins
Ground flaxseed	1 tablespoon ground flaxseed plus 3 tablespoons water, whipped up and then left to set for a few minutes (it gets thick like an egg white)	Things that are chewy, such as brownies and cookies, and also yeasted breads, especially sweet ones
Silken tofu	¼ cup, puréed	Cakes that are slightly dense in texture, pies, quick breads and muffins
Buttermilk	1 teaspoon mild vinegar (white or apple cider) plus enough milk to make ¼ cup	Cakes, quick breads and muffins; this is a hybrid leavener and binder, making things rise and stay moist
Assorted puréed/shredded fruits or veggies (like canned pumpkin, mashed banana, zucchini, carrots, or pears)	¼ cup; if your recipe already calls for fruits or veggies, you can typically take out the eggs and add 1 tablespoon of milk per egg to replace the liquid content	Quick breads, muffins, cakes
Ener-G egg replacer	See directions on box	This boxed egg-replacer is not my favorite, but it is easy to find and shelf stable. It is starch-based, so I don't recommend it for things that you want to stay really moist, such as cake.

When you are veganizing a recipe, you might find that you don't even need to pick a binder because there are already elements in the recipe binding it together, like in banana bread or pumpkin cookies. If you play around with the traditional versions of those recipes, you'll just need to add a little more liquid to make up for the lost moisture, as noted above, but it's easy to see that the eggs served no purpose at all!

You'll see throughout the book that I tend to stick to the same few binders. This is not because the other ones are bad, these are just my preferences. As you veganize your own recipes, don't despair if one substitute doesn't work out the first time. Give it a try with another one.

Look at all of these options! Silly omnivores, putting eggs in everything. It's like duct tape: Just because it can fix something doesn't mean it can fix everything. Just because eggs worked in something doesn't mean they are needed for everything, or frankly, anything! The only reason eggs seem "normal" and applesauce or flaxmeal seems "weird" is simply because it's what we are used to. So if you ever feel like putting a scoop of applesauce in your cookie dough is weird, just reflect on who in the world decided to put ovum in their cookie dough, and your cookies will taste all the sweeter.

To Milk or Not to Milk

As I refined this book, I truly agonized over the way to write about milk. I've seen vegan recipes that assume soy milk instead of milk, and I've seen recipes where milk is in quotes, with recipes calling for "milk." Now let's take a moment to think about coconut milk. No one protests calling that milk. Alternative milks date back hundreds and hundreds of years to different regions of the world, so they aren't a new invention, they are just newly recognized by our Western society. Because of my strong views on the linguistics of eating, I chose to simply use the word "milk." This is a vegan book, so clearly the use of animal milk is unintended. This also holds true in my use of the word "yogurt"; again, yogurt made from animal milk is not welcome here.

There are many different kinds of milk out there. The first one most people default to is soy. It's becoming so prominent that I've actually seen it at interstate gas stations!

COMMON CONVERSIONS

If you find you want to veganize a recipe that doesn't use standard U.S. measurements or you're in a kitchen filled with metric measuring tools, here are some handy conversions:

1 teaspoon	5 milliliters
1 tablespoon	15 milliliters
1 cup	240 milliliters
1 pint (2 cups)	470 milliliters
1 quart (4 cups)	.95 liter
1 gallon (4 quarts)	3.8 liters
1 fluid ounce	30 milliliters / 28 grams
1 ounce	28 grams
1 pound (16 ounces)	454 grams
350°F / 400°F	175°C / 200°C

But it's not the only milk option, and some people have sensitivities to soy. Rice, almond, oat, and hazelnut are all other milks I tried working with in this book. The only thing soy has on any of these other milks is that it has a higher fat content, which can be a bonus in some recipes, but is usually a moot point. I have recommended specific milks where they apply, but otherwise please feel free to use whatever milk you prefer. However, I don't recommend using coconut milk because it has a very high fat content, even in low-fat versions, and so it won't respond in a recipe the way regular milks will.

I normally buy milk in the shelf-stable aseptic boxes. Once opened, they need to be refrigerated, but until then you can stow them away in your pantry. When my husband and I first went vegan, we bought refrigerated soy milk, and the aseptic milks seemed so foreign that I was hesitant to try them. But now I find them to be far superior to the refrigerated versions in both taste and quality of ingredients. They are also wonderful because when your favorite milk is on sale you can stock up without worrying about approaching expiration dates.

Sugars and Sweeteners

What's not vegan about sugar? I mean, it's sweet, yummy and addictive like crack, but it's not that bad. Right? Well, to start with, traditional white sugar is refined with animal bone charcoal filters, so while the animal products aren't actually in it, they are used in its production. Plus, white sugar is bleached, and we want to try to avoid that. Cane sugar, like white sugar, is usually bleached with bone charcoal, but sugar derived from beets usually is not. If you have questions regarding the veganness of your sugar, I suggest contacting the company directly.

There are plenty of delicious sweeteners to use aside from white sugar. The easiest to find are organic sugar and evaporated cane juice. Organic sugar is cane sugar processed without the bone charcoal and bleach. It has a slightly more golden color than white sugar. Evaporated cane juice is made from cane juice that has been dehydrated and crystallized. You can use either of these blonde-colored sweeteners cup for cup when substituting for white sugar.

You can also find darker, less-processed sugars such as demarara, Sucanat or Sugar in the Raw. These are going to have a richer flavor, which is slightly caramelly because they still have some molasses in them.

You can find organic brown and powdered sugars as well. You can make your own brown sugar by mixing 1 tablespoon of molasses into each cup of sugar that you are using. You can freshen up old store-bought brown sugar that has hardened by putting a half piece of bread in the bag overnight. The brown sugar will absorb the moisture from the bread, and you'll be left with a giant, sweet-smelling crouton in the morning.

There are also many liquid sweeteners. These include agave nectar, maple syrup, brown rice syrup, corn syrup and molasses. With the exception of molasses, they can be pricey and difficult to find. These sweeteners taste great and can be fun to play with in your baking. Err on the side of caution when substituting a liquid sweetener for a dry one, however, as it will shift your recipe's liquid-to-solid ratio. You will have to cut back on the volume of sweetener that you use. Since substitution can be a tricky business, I usually stick to what is written when it comes to liquid versus solid ingredients. There are a couple of recipes in this book that call for liquid sweeteners, but I try to list alternative sweeteners as well. In some recipes I list things like "agave nectar or corn syrup" because corn syrup is cheaper and easier to find.

Sometimes you will see sugar listed with the wet ingredients in a recipe and sometimes you will see it listed with the dry. Why the difference? It depends on the recipe's liquid-to-solid ratio. In recipes like cookies, which have a low amount of liquids, it is used as a wet ingredient to make the liquids more evenly match the dry ingredients in volume. Sugar can naturally retain water and will technically increase the amount of wet ingredients, making it easier to mix in the dry. Combining it with the wet ingredients also helps it break down faster. Sometimes, however, sugar is a dry ingredient and is used to help break up another dry ingredient, like flour or cornstarch. For instance, in most cakes, sugar is used as a dry ingredient to help keep the flour from clumping and to help absorb the liquid ingredients more evenly. In this book, some of the recipes show the wet and dry ingredients separately to make the recipes easier to read. As a rule, though, always read the entire recipe to see what function the sugar serves and to get a feel for the recipe as a whole so there are no surprises once you really get into it.

The Skinny on Fat: Margarine, Shortening and Oil

Butter, butter, butter leaves the bowl! Baking without butter is easy as pie—pie with a flaky, crisp crust, made without any trace of butter at all, in fact. There are some wonderful commercial vegan margarines out there, including Earth Balance, Spectrum Naturals and Willow Run. I normally use Earth Balance, because it is widely available. I understand that finding these margarines is not always that easy, and in smaller towns or little co-op stores, it can be pretty pricey. In developing the recipes in this book, I sought out some "accidentally" vegan margarines to experiment with. While not all margarines are dairy-free (look for ingredients like whey), there are some commercially made margarines that are. Many of them have hydrogenated oils, but sometimes that's all that is available or affordable. I have experimented with baking with some of these margarines and am happy to report that in my own experiments, everything baked up just as it should have.

There are options out there for vegan shortening, too. Shortening is different from margarine (or butter for that matter) because it has a 100% fat content. It is fully solid at room temperature. Shortening was invented as a cheap vegetable-oil replacement for lard. Most shortenings originally had hydrogenated oils in them, which is what made them solid, but due to health concerns many brands are changing to nonhydrogenated oils and increasing the solid vegetable oils used in production. Shortening can usually be replaced by margarine, but it will affect the texture and sometimes the taste of a baked good. Earth Balance makes a shortening, and if you're in a pinch, good old Crisco is vegan, too. Always be sure that your shortening is room temperature unless otherwise stated, otherwise it will be far too hard to blend with other ingredients.

Oil is another fat used in baking. Oils that can withstand higher temperatures are the ones you want to bake with, so olive oil (except in small amounts in specific recipes) is out. You want to bake with an oil that is light and mild in flavor, such as vegetable or canola oil. It is possible in some recipes to substitute oil for margarine, but again you need to revisit your liquid-to-solid ratios. Margarines are solid at room temperature, whereas oils are not, so you will need less oil than you would margarine. In recipes such as quick breads, you can substitute oil for margarine (⅓ cup oil in place of ½ cup margarine) and usually have success, but for things like cookies, I wouldn't recommend it.

The Magical World of Leavening

In baking there are several different leaveners, which are elements that help make your baked goods rise and contribute to their overall structure and texture. Leaveners include baking soda, baking powder and yeast.

Baking Soda and Baking Powder: Separated at Birth?

Many people confuse baking soda and powder for one another, which is understandable. Baking soda is sodium bicarbonate. It is a base that relies on something acidic in your other ingredients to activate it. Sometimes it's something like apple cider vinegar, yogurt or cocoa, and other times it's just milk. This interaction creates carbon dioxide bubbles, which you may notice as soon as you combine the wet and dry ingredients. Baked goods with

COME FLY WITH ME...

The most important things to consider when baking for a package are the moisture content of the item (you want some moisture, but not too much) and how sturdy it is. Something as delicate as Pain au Chocolat isn't the best choice for long-distance travel!

Nothing says lovin' like a care package of baked goods! But what to bake... and how to send it?

You want to pick items that have a longer shelf life and you want to package them in a way that will keep them in one piece. For cookies, I usually opt for a cookie tin, lined with tissue paper and layers of cookies, with additional tissue paper crumpled on top to help cushion them. Muffins and breads can be baked in decorative liners, which you can find at many kitchen supply stores. Bake mini loaves of quick bread, wrap them in colorful cellophane and wrap them in a little bubble wrap. A little creativity and a good dose of padding goes a long way. Your loved ones will appreciate the gesture, and care packages filled with treats are sure to deliver smiles upon receipt!

baking soda must go from being mixed to being baked as quickly as possible so they do not fall flat.

Baking powder has some sodium bicarbonate in it, but it also contains its own acid. These elements come alive with the introduction of wet ingredients. Baking powder comes in two varieties: single-acting and double-acting. Single-acting is your regular store variety. It starts doing its job as soon as it comes in contact with moisture. The double-acting kind reacts partially to moisture and partially to heat, so it can hang out a bit longer before it needs to be baked. I tend to be wary of double-acting baking powder because of the chemical used to delay it: aluminum sulfate. You can, however, purchase baking powder that is labeled as "aluminum free."

So, if they both cause baked goods to rise, why have both? Ah, but there is reasoning for that, too. Baking soda is a hard worker, cranking out all of those little carbon dioxide bubbles, but it can become unstable when baked for long periods of time or at very high temperatures. Baking powder works a little more slowly and has more stability, which is why you often see them paired up, a super duo out to rid the world of flat, dense baked goods.

The Yeast Beast

Yeast can be rather scary if you've never baked with it before, but once you try it you'll wonder why you didn't sooner. It is important to make sure you are using baking yeast when baking. Many a sad story circulates on the internet of someone using nutritional yeast (which is solely a flavoring and nutritional agent) to try to make bread only to have their loaf fall.

Yeast is a bacteria that multiplies and creates carbon dioxide bubbles, which in turn raise your baked goods. The bacteria feed on starch in the food, which is why you will often see yeast "proofed" or activated with warm water and something sweet, like a bit of sugar or molasses. Once all the ingredients are combined, the yeast feeds off of the starch in the flour to multiply and rise. This is why white bread, which has much of the protein stripped out of it and is essentially a starch loaf, will rise more easily than hard wheat.

Yeast comes in two forms: dried (in packets in the baking section or jars in the refrigerated section of the grocery store) or fresh (as a cake, in the refrigerated section of your grocery store, but this is less commonly used). Once you've opened your yeast, whether it is fresh or dried, you should store the extra in the fridge. But always let it come to room temperature prior to using it. Also be sure to check the expiration date on your yeast. Fresh yeast cakes have a very short life, whereas packages can sometimes be kept for up to a year. Old yeast = no rising, so remember to check!

There are different kinds of dried yeast. Traditional yeast, often called "active dried," has larger granules, and you will see that most recipes call for this kind of yeast. It requires at least 1 to 2 hours for rising, so plan ahead. Fast rising, or "rapid-rise" yeast, which has smaller granules, can rise in half the time of traditional yeast, and is a time-saving alternative.

You may wonder who would bother with traditional yeast, then. I typically use traditional yeast when I'm going to be home for the day and can just let my bread rise slowly, or if I'm making a large meal and I need to plan out what time things are going to be done. Being able to give your bread a time slot can be helpful if you are spending the whole day in the kitchen. Fast rising is great when you are low on time. After working all day, I know that I can put together the dough for the Garlic Rolls (page 136) when I get in the door and they will be ready to pop in the oven and bake for dinner about an hour later. Just like how wine tastes different when it's aged, bread tastes different when it rises slowly rather than quickly, but it's all a matter of subtlety and preference. Figure out what suits your baking style and go with it; the results are worth it either way.

Is yeast vegan? This is a question that comes up because yeast is a bacteria, which can die, so technically it is alive. Yeast has no known central nervous system, brain or reproductive abilities. It's simply a bacterium that can rapidly clone itself, so it is not viewed as an actual animal and is therefore vegan.

Stocking Your Pantry

A good bulk foods section of a grocery store will help you fill your pantry with the elements to bake on a whim. I love being able to just pull out what I need to make some cookies after dinner or bake a quick cake whenever I feel like it. Use mason jars or small, tightly sealed storage containers to house ingredients that you buy in smaller quantities, such as specialty flours. This gives them a cool, dry place to live where you can easily find them so you don't have to rummage through a bunch of bulk food bags to find spelt flour, hoping that you labeled it clearly.

Here is what I like to keep around:

IN THE PANTRY:

AGAVE NECTAR

BAKING POWDER

BAKING SODA

CAROB CHIPS

CHOCOLATE CHIPS

DRIED FRUITS (CRANBERRIES, RAISINS, CHERRIES)

EXTRA MILKS

EXTRACTS (VANILLA, ALMOND, MINT)

MOLASSES

NUTRITIONAL YEAST

OAT BRAN

OATMEAL

ORGANIC SUGARS (OR EVAPORATED CANE JUICE)

ORGANIC POWDERED SUGAR

SALT

SPICES AND DRIED HERBS (CINNAMON, PUMPKIN PIE SPICE, OREGANO)

UNBLEACHED ALL-PURPOSE FLOUR

WHITE WHOLE-WHEAT FLOUR

WHOLE-WHEAT PASTRY FLOUR

YEAST, TRADITIONAL AND RAPID-RISE

IN THE FRIDGE/FREEZER:

APPLE CIDER VINEGAR

APPLESAUCE

FROZEN BERRIES

GROUND FLAXSEED (GROUND FLAXSEED ALWAYS NEEDS TO BE REFRIGERATED, BUT I RECOMMEND GRINDING YOUR OWN FROM WHOLE SEEDS FOR BEST RESULTS)

LEMON JUICE

MAPLE SYRUP

OIL SUITABLE FOR BAKING AND COOKING (I USUALLY USE CANOLA FOR BAKING AND OLIVE OR GRAPESEED OIL FOR COOKING)

SOY YOGURT

VEGAN MARGARINE

Tools & Tips For Success

The following are some of the tools and tricks that I feel are important for successful baking. Some are more important than others, but they are all things I've found helpful to improve the quality of my baking.

INSULATED COOKIE SHEETS   I will never again bake cookies on a cookie sheet that isn't insulated. They have become relatively easy to find, and they're cheap, too, which is why I encourage everyone to have at least one insulated cookie sheet. They consist of two metal sheets with a layer of air between them. The air allows the sheet to heat evenly, providing evenly baked cookies that are also softer than those baked on a conventional cookie sheet.

UNBLEACHED PARCHMENT PAPER   I bake almost everything on parchment paper. It serves several wonderful purposes. First, it means that you don't have to grease anything. No more prying cookies up with a spatula only to have them crumble and break apart. Nope, your cookies will come off effortlessly and in one piece with no dark brown bottoms. You can use a simple sheet of it to cover a cookie sheet, you can cut it to fit into the bottom of a round cake pan (just place the pan on top of the paper, trace and cut out) or you can fit it into a pan for easy brownie removal. It also makes cleanup simple and, with cookie sheets, effortless. Simply throw out the parchment paper and you can put your cookie sheet away! It feels strange to endorse something that is disposable, but you can use the same sheet several times. You tear off a sheet and bake a couple dozen cookies, then turn it over and make home fries for dinner and you won't need to coat them in oil.

MELTING CHOCOLATE

Melting chocolate requires a little technique, but once you get the hang of it, it's very easy and you will have a consistently creamy product. The most important point to melting chocolate is that it be done slowly.

The two best ways of melting chocolate are either in a double boiler or in the microwave. A double boiler is a pot that gets suspended above a pot with water in it. The water in the bottom pot gets heated on the stove top and its steam heats up the pot of chocolate above it, slowly melting it. You can make a makeshift double boiler by using a small pot of water with a glass or ceramic bowl suspended over it. Be sure that the water does not touch the bottom of the bowl.

You can also melt it in the microwave. Chocolate that is melted in the microwave should always be chopped up and microwaved in small 10–12 second zaps, stirred after each time.

Whichever method you use, you must take care to stir constantly. Chocolate is a bit mischievous and will retain what appears to be a solid shape even when it is liquefied inside, so it's very important to stir it frequently so it doesn't burn. If you are adding something to chocolate after it is melted, it is important that it be room temperature, never cold. This will cause the chocolate to seize up, making it thick and lumpy. The same is true to adding water of any temperature to chocolate. If you want to thin out chocolate, always use a room temperature milk.

Now, don't be afraid to melt chocolate if this sounds like too much pressure. I assure you, it's simple. You just need to use a careful eye.

COOLING RACKS   It's worth the investment to buy a few cooling racks so you can transition your baked goods from the hot oven to let them cool. Leaving them in the pan, sitting on a stove burner is just asking for trouble. It's important to remember that even when you take something out of the oven, it continues baking on the inside, and if it's on a hot pan, well, your cookies are going to be well-done. Most recipes will include cooling directions, and they are just as important as the baking ones. Letting your baked goods cool in the pan on a cooling rack for the recommended amount of time and then transitioning them to another cooling rack is the best way to have evenly baked food.

FOOD PROCESSOR   Yes, I know it's a little bit of an investment, but it pays off in so many ways. I use my food processor weekly, not just for baking but for tons of other kinds of food prep. It makes cooking and baking so easy that once you go processor, you'll never go back.

GLASS BAKING PANS   The darker your pan, the darker the outside of your baked goods. Using glass ensures that your brownies will not be blackened when they come out of the oven.

OVEN THERMOMETER   If you think your oven temperature is accurate... think again. Some ovens are great, others are a little off. Mine likes to tell me that it's done preheating when it's still about 50 degrees off. Thermometers are inexpensive and a great way to make sure your oven is operating correctly.

SIFTER   You can pick a sifter up on the cheap at many stores. A sifter is invaluable when making frosting or icing, as powdered sugar tends to clump. Once you have one, you'll be amazed how often you use it.

ELECTRIC HAND MIXER   A good electric hand mixer is priceless for making cake batter and frosting.

You May Ask Yourself, "How Do I Use This Book?"

- Recipes have a difficulty rating from 1 to 5, with 1 being very simple and 5 being challenging. The ratings also take into account if a recipe is involved and requires more preparation than others. Don't be afraid to try harder ones—you will surprise yourself!
- Be sure to read each recipe completely before you start, because you never know if there will be a curve ball.
- All references to flour refer to unbleached all-purpose flour unless otherwise stated.
- All references to sugar mean regular granulated sugar, unless otherwise noted. I normally bake with organic cane sugar, but I also use evaporated cane juice, which can be substituted 1 to 1 for regular sugar.
- All references to silken tofu refer to the aseptic boxed, sealed tofu (not the water-packed kind). These little boxes are similar to the aseptic milks in that they do not have to be refrigerated and may be found either on the shelf or in the refrigerated section at the grocery store. The most common brand name is Mori-Nu and each box is 12.3 ounces, but you may find other brands that are labeled as "silken" in different sizes. Silken tofu is becoming increasingly easier to find, especially in the Asian food section of your grocery store.
- All references to milk in this book refer to any vegan milk of your choice, unless a specific vegan milk is noted. This is a vegan cookbook, so naturally I mean vegan milk.
- All references to baking cocoa mean the pure cocoa used for baking, not hot cocoa mix.

- All references to yogurt mean plain or vanilla soy yogurt.
- All references to oil refer to a mild vegetable oil, unless otherwise noted. This means something light and mild, such as vegetable or canola oil. Never bake with large quantities of olive oil; it is a low-temperature oil and does not do well in baked goods.
- All references to cornstarch can be replaced with arrowroot starch.
- All references to peanut butter refer to natural peanut butter, which is normally just peanuts and sometimes oil, not commercial peanut butter with additives.
- Prep and baking times are provided to help you plan ahead.
- When checking a baked good using a toothpick, always check near the center of the item to check the consistency. "Coming out clean" means that there is no liquid batter or dough on the toothpick. With moist items, such as cake, there may be little crumbs that stick, but the toothpick shouldn't be coated.

The two best tips for baking that I can give you are:

1. Always read through the entire recipe before starting to bake. You never know if a recipe is going to be a little different than you are expecting, and no one likes to be surprised.

   and

2. Have fun! Baking is a blast, almost as much of one as actually eating the results. Put on some music, grab an apron and enjoy the ride.

COOKIES

If I were trapped on a desert island and could have only one kind of baked good with me, it would be cookies. Well, first I would lobby for a dessert island rather than a desert island, but if I couldn't get that second s, I would be happy with the cookies. From experienced pastry chefs to beginning bakers, everyone loves cookies. They are flexible (with add-ins such as nuts or chocolate chips), they are hand-held and they are a cinch to whip up. What's not to love?

- CHOCOLATE CHIP PECAN COOKIES
- LEMON DROP COOKIES
- SHORTBREAD
- CHOCOLATE PEANUT BUTTER SHELLS
- SNICKERDOODLES
- PEANUT BUTTER COOKIES
- CHEWY CHOCOLATE-PEPPERMINT COOKIES
- OATMEAL DRIZZLES
- MOCHA STRIPES
- APPLE BUTTER COOKIES
- SPICE-SPIKED CHOCOLATE CHUNK COOKIES
- PUMPKIN CHOCOLATE CHIP COOKIES
- CHOCOLATE CHERRY-FILLED COOKIES
- HIPPY DIPPY CRACKERS

CHOCOLATE CHIP PECAN COOKIES

Hate nuts? Leave 'em out! Pecans add a twist to these classic treats, and they're everything you want from a chocolate chip cookie—chewy edges, a soft middle and warm, chocolatey goodness.

2 cups flour

1 teaspoon baking soda

¼ teaspoon salt

1 cup margarine, softened

½ cup sugar

½ cup brown sugar, packed

1 teaspoon vanilla

1 teaspoon cornstarch

2 tablespoons milk

½ cup chocolate chips

½ cup chopped pecans

. . . .

Want warm cookies anytime? This dough stores well in your fridge for up to a week. Just scoop out a couple at a time to have fresh cookies after dinner!

Preheat the oven to 350 degrees. Line baking sheets with parchment paper.

In a large bowl, whisk together flour, baking soda and salt. In a separate large bowl, cream together sugar, brown sugar and margarine. Dissolve cornstarch in milk and add to sugar mixture along with vanilla. Add flour mixture to sugar mixture in batches, then stir in chocolate chips and pecans.

Using a cookie dropper or tablespoon, drop heaping tablespoons of dough onto baking sheet, about 2 inches apart. Bake for 8 to 10 minutes, or until edges are slightly golden. If you are baking more than one sheet at a time, rotate the sheets about halfway through the baking time. Remove cookies from the oven and let cool on the baking sheet for 5 minutes, then transfer to a cooling rack. Store cooled cookies in an airtight container at room temperature.

Yield: 2½ DOZEN COOKIES
Prep time: 20 MINUTES
Difficulty:

LEMON DROP COOKIES

When I first went to college, I basically lived off of powdered sugar–coated lemon wafer cookies that were made by a major cookie manufacturer. Naturally, because I liked them, they stopped making them about a year after I got hooked, and I spent nearly a decade feeling sorry for myself before realizing that I didn't care about their silly cookies—I could make my own! These little cookies are crisp and tart; the powdered sugar takes the edge off and adds a sweet coolness to each bite.

½ cup margarine, softened

½ cup shortening, at room temperature

¾ cup sugar

2 teaspoons lemon zest

juice of 1 lemon

2 cups flour

1½ cups powdered sugar, for coating

· ·

For best results, zest the lemon before juicing. You can use the small holes on a grater for a fine zest.

Preheat the oven to 375 degrees. Line a baking sheet with parchment paper.

In a large bowl, cream together margarine and shortening until smooth. Mix in sugar to combine, then incorporate lemon zest and juice. Add flour in small batches until well-incorporated.

Drop teaspoon-sized balls of dough onto a baking sheet, about 1 inch apart. Bake for 8 to 10 minutes until edges are set and slightly browned. If you are baking more than one sheet at a time, rotate the sheets about halfway through the baking time. Remove the cookies from the oven and let cool completely on the baking sheet before coating each cookie in powdered sugar. To coat, use a fork to support each cookie and roll them in powdered sugar on both sides. Store cooled cookies in an airtight container at room temperature.

Yield: 2½ DOZEN COOKIES
Prep time: 20 MINUTES
Difficulty:

SHORTBREAD

I usually prefer soft and chewy cookies, but there's just something about the crisp butteriness of shortbread that gets me. I usually top each cookie with some almond slivers before baking them, but they are also delicious plain. Be sure to plan ahead for these cookies, because the dough needs to chill in the fridge.

1 cup margarine, softened
¾ cup sugar, divided
1 teaspoon vanilla
2¼ cups flour

. . . .

Make this dough the night before so all you have to do is slice and bake.

In a large bowl, cream together margarine, ½ cup sugar and vanilla until well-combined. Add flour in batches and mix until dough is soft and smooth. Divide dough in half and shape each half into a log about 6 inches long by 2 inches wide. Wrap each log in plastic wrap and refrigerate for at least 2 hours.

Preheat the oven to 375 degrees. Line baking sheets with parchment paper.

Remove logs from the fridge and roll each log in the remaining sugar, to coat. Using a sharp knife, cut logs into ¼-inch thick slices, rolling the log as you cut to maintain its shape. Place sliced cookies on the baking sheets and decorate them with dried fruit or nuts, if you want. Bake for 8 minutes or until edges are lightly browned. If you are baking more than one sheet at a time, rotate the sheets halfway through the baking time. Remove cookies from the oven and let cool for 5 minutes, then transfer to a cooling rack. Store cooled cookies in an airtight container at room temperature.

Yield: 2 DOZEN
Prep time: 20 MINUTES ACTIVE
Difficulty: ✎

Chocolate Peanut Butter Shells

This is undoubtedly my most requested cookie recipe and it's my personal favorite treat. Originally, my sister gave me a recipe similar to this one. After becoming addicted to these cookies, I lost the original recipe and I needed it ASAP for an event I was baking for, so I had to do some improvising and call on my rusty memory and some random notes I had once scribbled down about them. The result? An even better version of the original cookie. These are a little time consuming but so, so worth it.

DOUGH:

1½ cups flour

½ cup baking cocoa

½ teaspoon baking soda

½ cup margarine, softened

½ cup sugar

½ cup brown sugar, packed

¼ cup milk

1 teaspoon vanilla

FILLING:

¾ to 1 cup sifted powdered sugar

½ cup peanut butter

⅓ cup chocolate chips

¼ teaspoon coarse salt

Preheat the oven to 350 degrees. Line a baking sheet with parchment paper.

For Dough: In a small bowl, sift together flour, cocoa and baking soda. In a large bowl, beat together margarine, sugar and brown sugar. Add milk and vanilla to the sugar mixture. Beat well. Gently mix in the flour mixture about ⅓ at a time until incorporated. The dough should have a texture similar to Play-Doh.

For Filling: Combine peanut butter and ½ cup powdered sugar in a mixing bowl; keep adding remaining powdered sugar and beat until sugar is absorbed and peanut butter feels stiff and no longer appears shiny. Stir in chocolate chips. It should be a pretty solid mixture because you want to form it into little balls.

Take a piece of dough just a bit smaller than the size of a golf ball and flatten it into a disc on a piece of parchment paper. Place a heaping teaspoon of the peanut butter mixture on the center of the dough. Carefully fold the chocolate dough over the peanut butter ball and seal the edges. If the dough cracks, you can easily pinch it back together. Roll the dough into a ball.

Place balls on the baking sheet, 1 inch apart, sealed side down. Bake for about 8 minutes, until cookies begin to crack slightly on the surface. Let cool for 1 minute on the baking sheet, then carefully transfer to a cooling rack. Store cooled cookies in an airtight container at room temperature.

Yield: 1½ DOZEN COOKIES

Prep time: 45 MINUTES

Difficulty:

SNICKERDOODLES

The cinnamon-sugar coating is a simple comfort that has a timeless appeal.

2½ cups flour
2 teaspoons baking powder
¼ teaspoon salt
1¾ cups sugar, divided
½ cup margarine, softened
¼ cup applesauce
½ teaspoon vanilla
2 tablespoons cinnamon

· ·

For a different twist, add 3 tablespoons of baking cocoa to the flour mixture at the beginning of the recipe for a Mexican chocolate–inspired treat!

Preheat the oven to 375 degrees. Line two baking sheets with parchment paper.

In a medium bowl, whisk together flour, baking powder and salt. In a large bowl, cream together margarine and 1½ cups sugar. Add applesauce and vanilla and mix until well blended. Add dry ingredients to wet ingredients in batches and mix until well-combined.

On a plate, combine cinnamon and remaining ¼ cup sugar. Scoop out tablespoon-sized balls of dough and roll them in cinnamon-sugar mixture and place on baking sheets, about 1 inch apart. Bake cookies for 8 to 10 minutes, until they have cracked and spread and the edges are set. If you are baking more than one sheet at a time, rotate their sheets halfway through the baking time. Let cookies cool on the baking sheets for 10 minutes, then transfer to a cooling rack. Store cooled cookies in an airtight container at room temperature.

Yield: 2 DOZEN COOKIES
Prep time: 25 MINUTES
Difficulty: 🥄

PEANUT BUTTER COOKIES

This was adapted from my great-grandmother's recipe, which none of us even knew she had. I found it in an old cookbook her church put out in the '70s. Unlike most peanut butter cookies, these are very soft and chewy, not hard or crumbly. Add a ½ cup of chocolate chips for warm cookie bliss.

2 cups flour, sifted
2 teaspoons baking soda
¼ teaspoon salt
1 cup margarine, softened
1 cup sugar
1 cup brown sugar, packed
¼ cup applesauce
1 teaspoon vanilla
1 cup peanut butter

. . . .

Other nut butters are great in this recipe. Try almond or cashew—subtle but divine!

Preheat the oven to 350 degrees. Line baking sheets with parchment paper.

In a small bowl, combine flour, baking soda and salt. In a large bowl, cream together margarine, sugar, brown sugar, applesauce and vanilla. Add peanut butter and mix well; this may require a hand mixer or some electric beaters at a slow speed. Add dry ingredients to wet ingredients and blend until just mixed.

Drop heaping tablespoon-sized balls of dough onto baking sheet, about 2 inches apart. These cookies spread very nicely, but you can press them with a fork for that classic peanut butter cookie look. Bake for 10 minutes, or until tops crack slightly and edges are a little browned. If you are baking more than one sheet at a time, rotate the sheets halfway through the baking time. Let the cookies cool on the baking sheet for 10 minutes, then transfer to a cooling rack. Store cooled cookies in an airtight container at room temperature.

Yield: 2 DOZEN COOKIES
Prep time: 20 MINUTES
Difficulty:

CHEWY CHOCOLATE-PEPPERMINT COOKIES

Chocolate and peppermint have their own special love affair going on, not unlike chocolate and peanut butter. These cookies are chocolatey and chewy with the right hint of mint—yum!

1 cup flour
½ cup baking cocoa
½ teaspoon baking soda
¼ teaspoon salt
¼ cup chocolate chips, melted
½ cup margarine, softened
1 cup sugar
2 tablespoons ground flaxseed
¼ cup milk
1 teaspoon vanilla
1 recipe for Peppermint Icing
(page 159)

. . . .

You can add a drop of green food coloring to the icing if you want your cookies to look festive, or you can add sprinkles to the cookies before the icing sets up.

. . . .

If you've never melted chocolate before, see note on page 26.

Preheat the oven to 325 degrees. Line two baking sheets with parchment paper.

In a medium bowl, sift together flour, cocoa, baking soda and salt. In a large bowl, cream together melted chocolate chips, margarine and sugar until well-combined. Add ground flaxseed, milk and vanilla and mix for 1 minute with an electric hand mixer on low speed. Add dry ingredients to wet ingredients in batches until fully incorporated.

Scoop teaspoon-sized balls of dough onto baking sheets, about 1 inch apart. Bake for 15 minutes or until edges are set. If you are baking more than one sheet at a time, rotate the sheets halfway through the baking time. Let cookies cool on the sheet for 5 minutes, then transfer to a cooling rack. While cookies are cooling, prepare the Peppermint Icing. When cookies are completely cool, spread a thin layer of icing on top. Store cooled cookies in an airtight container at room temperature.

Yield: 2 DOZEN COOKIES
Prep time: 30 MINUTES
Difficulty: 🥢🥢

OATMEAL DRIZZLES

These oatmeal cookies are chewy and soft, even after they cool. Dried cherries add a special flavor and a little icing drizzle makes these cookies top notch. These are "palmer" cookies, the kind that people try to hide in the palm of their hand so it only looks like they are taking one when they are really sneaking off with two or more!

1 cup flour

½ teaspoon baking soda

½ teaspoon cinnamon

⅛ teaspoon salt

½ cup plus 2 tablespoons margarine, softened

½ cup sugar

½ cup packed brown sugar

1 teaspoon vanilla

1 cup quick oats

½ cup dried tart cherries

1 recipe White Icing (page 155)

. . . .

For a delicious variation, try adding raisins instead of cherries and 2 teaspoons of orange zest.

Preheat the oven to 350 degrees. Line baking sheets with parchment paper.

In a small bowl, sift together flour, baking soda, cinnamon and salt. In a large bowl, cream together margarine, sugar, brown sugar and vanilla. Add flour mixture to sugar mixture. Add oatmeal in batches, and then stir in cherries.

Drop heaping tablespoon-sized cookies on baking sheets, about 3 inches apart. Bake for 11 to 14 minutes or until cookies are set in the center and the edges are lightly browned. If you are baking more than one sheet at a time, rotate the sheets halfway through the baking time. Cool on the baking sheet for 5 minutes, then transfer to a cooling rack. After the cookies are completely cool, drizzle them with White Icing and let icing set. Store cooled cookies in an airtight container at room temperature.

Yield: 2 DOZEN COOKIES
Prep time: 25 MINUTES
Difficulty:

Mocha Stripes

Chocolate is an equal-opportunity lover. It pairs famously with peanut butter. It embraces fruit and preserves. But it dances with coffee, which makes sense since both of them come from tropical beans that are roasted to perfection. These cookies are a perfect pairing of the two and will make you feel grown-up even if you have melted chocolate on your hands.

2 cups flour

1 teaspoon baking powder

½ teaspoon salt

4 tablespoon instant coffee

¼ cup warm milk

¾ cup margarine

1½ cups sugar

1 teaspoon vanilla

½ cup chocolate chips, melted

. . . .

If you've never melted chocolate before, see note on page 26.

Preheat the oven to 350 degrees. Line baking sheets with parchment paper.

In a medium bowl, sift together flour, baking powder and salt. In a small bowl, dissolve coffee in warm milk. In a large bowl, cream together margarine and sugar. Add vanilla and coffee mixture. Add dry ingredients to wet ingredients in batches until well-mixed.

Drop tablespoon-sized balls onto a baking sheet, about 1 inch apart. Bake for 10 minutes until the cookies spread and the edges are set. If you are baking more than one sheet at a time, rotate the sheets halfway through the baking time. Let cookies cool for 5 minutes on the baking sheet before transferring to a cooling rack.

Once the cookies are cool, carefully spoon melted chocolate into a sandwich bag. Make a small snip off one of the bottom corners of the bag to create a very small opening. Pipe chocolate onto cookies in thin stripes, zig-zagging across all the cookies until the chocolate is used up. Store cooled cookies in an airtight container at room temperature.

Yield: 2 DOZEN COOKIES

Prep time: 20 MINUTES

Difficulty:

APPLE BUTTER COOKIES

The apple butter in these cookies just screams autumn. I have never brought these to a potluck without getting at least one recipe request. I usually make these with 1 cup all-purpose flour and 1 cup whole-wheat pastry flour.

2 cups flour
1 teaspoon baking powder
½ teaspoon baking soda
1 teaspoon cinnamon
¼ teaspoon ground ginger
¼ teaspoon salt
1 cup margarine, softened
½ cup sugar
½ cup brown sugar, packed
¾ cup apple butter
1 teaspoon vanilla

. . . .

Dried raisins or cranberries are a great treat to add to these for extra texture and flavor!

Preheat the oven to 350 degrees. Line baking sheets with parchment paper.

In a small bowl, sift together flour, baking powder, baking soda, cinnamon, ginger and salt. In a large bowl, use a whisk or an electric hand mixer on a low speed to beat sugar, brown sugar and margarine until creamy. Add apple butter and vanilla. Add dry ingredients to wet ingredients in two batches and mix until well-combined.

Drop rounded tablespoonfuls onto baking sheets, 2 inches apart. Bake for 10 to 12 minutes or until the edges look slightly browned. If you are baking more than one sheet at a time, rotate the sheets halfway through the baking time. Cool cookies on the baking sheet for 5 minutes, then transfer to cooling rack. Store cooled cookies in an airtight container at room temperature.

Yield: 2 DOZEN
Prep time: 25 MINUTES
Difficulty:

Spice-Spiked Chocolate Chunk Cookies

Spices are too good to be relegated for holiday baking only. Have Christmas in July and fill your house with their aromatic scent! The crunch of the sugary coating and the chewy inside paired with the spicy flavor and dark chocolate is intoxicating.

2 cups flour

1 teaspoon baking powder

½ teaspoon baking soda

1 teaspoon ground ginger

1 teaspoon cinnamon

¼ teaspoon nutmeg

¼ teaspoon salt

¾ cup margarine, softened

½ cup plus 3 tablespoons sugar, divided

½ cup brown sugar, packed

2 tablespoons molasses

1 tablespoon milk

½ teaspoon vanilla

½ cup chopped dark chocolate bar

3 tablespoons sugar

Preheat the oven to 350 degrees. Line baking sheets with parchment paper.

In a medium bowl, combine flour, baking powder, baking soda, ginger, cinnamon, nutmeg and salt. In a large bowl, cream together margarine, ½ cup sugar and brown sugar. Add molasses, milk and vanilla. Add dry ingredients to wet ingredients in batches until well-incorporated. Add chopped chocolate.

Scoop out cookie dough into large tablespoon-sized balls and roll in remaining 3 tablespoons of sugar to coat. Place about 1 inch apart on a baking sheet and flatten slightly. Bake 8 to 10 minutes, until cookies have spread and sugar coating has cracked slightly. If you are baking more than one sheet at a time, rotate the sheets halfway through the baking time. Let cookies cool on the baking sheets for 10 minutes, then transfer to a cooling rack. Store cooled cookies in an airtight container at room temperature.

Yield: 2 DOZEN COOKIES
Prep time: 25 MINUTES
Difficulty:

PUMPKIN CHOCOLATE CHIP COOKIES

Always a favorite during the colder months, these cookies are very light and airy. The pumpkin adds a unique hue and a boost of beta carotene to each bite. That's enough nutrition to justify having seconds!

2 cups flour
1 teaspoon baking powder
1 teaspoon baking soda
1 teaspoon cinnamon
⅛ teaspoon salt
1 cup margarine, softened
½ cup sugar
½ cup brown sugar, packed
1 cup canned pumpkin
(not pumpkin pie filling)
1 teaspoon vanilla
½ cup chocolate chips

Preheat the oven to 350 degrees. Line baking sheets with parchment paper.

In a small bowl, combine flour, baking powder, baking soda, cinnamon and salt. In a large bowl, cream sugar, brown sugar and margarine with an electric hand mixer on low speed. Add pumpkin, vanilla and milk and mix well. Add flour mixture to sugar mixture, then stir in chocolate chips.

Drop heaping tablespoons of dough on baking sheets, 2 inches apart. Bake for 10 to 12 minutes or until cookies are lightly browned on the edges. If you are baking more than one sheet at a time, rotate the sheets halfway through the baking time. Let cookies cool on the baking sheet for 15 minutes, then transfer to a cooling rack. Store cooled cookies in a container with a loose fitting lid, as they are very moist, at room temperature.

Yield: 3 DOZEN COOKIES
Prep time: 25 MINUTES
Difficulty:

CHOCOLATE CHERRY-FILLED COOKIES

These cookies are a little labor intensive as cookies go, but they are well worth it. They are kind of the complement to Chocolate Peanut Butter Shells, the yin to their yang. These are what I like to think of as "surprise-attack" cookies—very unassuming-looking with a surprise filling that comes out of nowhere and shocks your unsuspecting mouth.

2 cups flour
1 teaspoon baking powder
¼ teaspoon salt
1 cup sugar
½ cup margarine, softened
½ teaspoon vanilla
2 tablespoons milk
½ cup chocolate chips
½ cup dried cherries
about 1 cup powdered sugar, for coating

Preheat the oven to 350 degrees. Line baking sheets with parchment paper.

In a small bowl, combine flour, baking powder and salt. In a large bowl, cream together sugar and margarine. Add vanilla and milk. Incorporate dry ingredients into wet ingredients in two batches until dough comes together. In a small bowl, combine chocolate chips and cherries. Put powdered sugar on a small plate.

Scoop out balls of dough approximately 2 tablespoons in size. Flatten balls in the palm of your hand and fill with 1 to 2 teaspoons of the chocolate chip mixture. Fold over edges to seal and roll into a ball. Roll cookies in powdered sugar and place seam-side down on baking sheets, about 1 inch apart. Bake for 9 to 11 minutes, until cookies are cracked on top and look slightly browned. If you are baking more than one sheet at once, rotate the sheets halfway through the baking time. Let cool on the baking sheet. Store cooled cookies in an airtight container at room temperature.

Yield: ABOUT 18 TO 24 COOKIES, DEPENDING ON SIZE
Prep time: 35 MINUTES
Difficulty:

HIPPY DIPPY CRACKERS

These seed-studded crackers are perfect for dunking into a soup or stew or for serving with hummus or some other dip. Have fun cutting out whatever shape or size your heart desires. The seeds in these crackers provide lots of healthy perks: Sesame seeds are high in calcium, flaxseeds are high in omegas and pumpkin seeds are high in iron.

1½ cups whole-wheat flour
1 cup all-purpose flour
⅓ cup oil
1 cup water
½ cup pumpkin seeds
¼ cup flaxseeds
¼ cup sesame seeds
sea salt, for sprinkling

Preheat the oven to 375 degrees. Line a large baking sheet with parchment paper.

In a large bowl, combine whole-wheat flour and all-purpose flour. Make a well in the middle of the flour mixture and add oil, water, pumpkin seeds, flaxseeds and sesame seeds and mix until well-combined. You can begin stirring with a spatula, but you may need to use your hands. The dough should be moist but not too sticky.

On a lightly floured surface, roll out dough to between $1/8$- and $1/16$-inch thick, depending on how thick you want your crackers to be. Transfer dough to the prepared baking sheet. Once dough is on the sheet, score the lines for your crackers using a knife or pizza cutter, but do not separate them. Lightly brush the top of the dough with water and sprinkle with sea salt, as desired.

Bake for 20 to 25 minutes or until crackers are browned and firm in the center. They do not need to be crispy yet, as they will harden up as they cool. Let crackers cool on the baking sheet on a cooling rack for 5 minutes before cutting crackers apart on score lines. Let cool completely before eating. Store crackers covered at room temperature.

Yield: ABOUT 2 DOZEN CRACKERS
Prep time: 25 MINUTES
Difficulty:

BARS

I am a Midwestern girl, so if it has four sides, it's called a bar, no ifs, ands or buts about it. You can call them squares if you'd like, but if you want to honor the artistic integrity of these recipes, you must pronounce "bars" with a really wide "ah" sound and a very distinct "ar" (think "Fargo") or the whole thing is just lost.

- GOOEY LAYERED GOODIE BARS
- OH JOE'S BROWNIES
- THE ULTIMATE BROWNIES
- CRANBERRY LEMON ZING OAT BARS
- LIME COCONUT BARS
- MOCHA-DAMIA BARS
- PEANUT BUTTER AND JELLY BARS
- OATMEAL EARTH BARS
- NUTS FOR CAROB BARS
- APRICOT BARS
- FUDGY MACAROON BARS

Gooey Layered Goodie Bars

No Midwestern potluck is complete without 7 Layer Bars. You can't escape them, no matter where you go. Not quite seven layers, these are my grown-up answer to 7 Layer Bars and all their gooey goodness.

BASE:

1¾ cups flour

1 teaspoon baking powder

¼ teaspoon salt

1 cup sugar

½ cup margarine

½ cup plus 2 tablespoons plain or vanilla yogurt
(equivalent to 1 6-ounce container)

1 teaspoon vanilla

TOPPING:

¼ cup brown sugar

1 tablespoon molasses

¼ cup milk

¾ cup nuts
(walnuts or pecans are best)

¾ cup chocolate chips

¾ cup dried fruit

⅓ cup dried coconut

· ·

Chopped dried apricots are wonderful in these bars, as are banana chips!

Preheat the oven to 350 degrees. Grease an 8 x 8-inch pan with margarine or oil, or line it with parchment paper.

For Base: In a small bowl, combine flour, baking powder and salt. In a medium bowl, cream together sugar and margarine until smooth. Add yogurt and vanilla to combine. Add dry ingredients to wet ingredients in batches until incorporated. Press mixture into the bottom of the prepared pan.

For Topping: In a small bowl, combine brown sugar, molasses and milk until well-mixed. Stir in nuts and chocolate chips until combined. Spread mixture over bar base.

Bake for 30 minutes, sprinkle coconut on top and bake for an additional 5 to 8 minutes until edges are set and coconut is slightly browned. Let bars cool in the pan on a cooling rack for 30 minutes before cutting. Store bars covered at room temperature.

Yield: 9 GENEROUS BARS

Prep time: 20 MINUTES

Difficulty:

OH JOE'S BROWNIES

A couple of years ago, I picked up a box of brownie mix from a certain specialty grocer that you probably shop at yourself. I looked at the ingredient list and was surprised at its simplicity, and I set about the task of cracking its code. The result is this simple recipe that results in a cakelike brownie full of chocolatey goodness.

1 cup sugar
¾ cup flour
⅓ cup baking cocoa
½ teaspoon salt
2 teaspoons baking powder
½ cup margarine, melted
½ cup plus 2 tablespoons plain or vanilla yogurt
(equal to 1 6-ounce container)
½ cup chocolate chips

Preheat the oven to 350 degrees. Lightly grease an 8 x 8-inch pan with margarine or oil, or line it with parchment paper.

In a small bowl, whisk sugar, flour, baking cocoa, salt and baking powder. In a large bowl, stir together margarine and yogurt. Add dry ingredients to wet ingredients in batches and mix until combined. Stir in chocolate chips.

Spread mixture in the prepared pan and bake for 30 to 35 minutes, until edges are set and a toothpick inserted into the center comes out clean. Let cool in the pan on a cooling rack for at least 30 minutes before cutting. Store brownies covered at room temperature.

Yield: 9 BROWNIES
Prep time: 25 MINUTES
Difficulty: 🥄

THE ULTIMATE BROWNIES

Why have two brownie recipes? Well, some folks like cakelike brownies while others prefer fudgy brownies, so everyone wins with two recipes! The whipped flaxseed gives these that flaky crust on top. These brownies depend on everything being prepared in a specific order, so read through the recipe thoroughly for successful results.

¾ cup flour

¼ teaspoon baking powder

¼ teaspoon salt

6 tablespoons margarine

⅓ cup plus ½ cup chocolate chips, divided

¼ cup baking cocoa

2 tablespoons ground flaxseed

⅓ cup water

1 cup sugar

2 teaspoons vanilla

Preheat the oven to 350 degrees. Lightly grease an 8 × 8-inch baking pan with margarine or oil, or line it with parchment paper.

In a small bowl, sift together flour, baking powder and salt; set aside.

In a heat-resistant bowl over a pot of simmering water, melt margarine, ⅓ cup chocolate chips and baking cocoa. The water should be about 1 to 2 inches deep and the bowl should not touch it. Stir until smooth and let cool slightly.

In a large bowl, mix ground flaxseed and water with an electric hand mixer for about 2 minutes or until mixture is very frothy and texture seems a little gooey. Add chocolate mixture and beat well. Add sugar and vanilla and mix until little air bubbles start rising to the top of the mixture. Add dry ingredients to wet ingredients then stir in remaining ½ cup chocolate chips and mix until well-combined.

Spread batter into the prepared pan and bake for 30 to 35 minutes or until a toothpick inserted into the center comes out clean and brownies have a thin, flakey crust on top. Let cool in the pan on a cooling rack for at least 30 minutes before cutting. Store brownies covered at room temperature.

Yield: 9 BARS
Prep time: 35 MINUTES
Difficulty:

CRANBERRY LEMON ZING OAT BARS

These bars were inspired by a seasonal treat at a world-famous coffee chain. I honestly don't know what theirs taste like (seeing as it's not vegan and all), but these are some darn good bars, with a chewy base speckled with tart cranberries and a creamy lemon frosting.

1½ cups flour
1 cup quick oats
½ teaspoon baking powder
½ teaspoon cinnamon
¼ teaspoon salt
1 cup sugar
¾ cup margarine, softened
½ cup applesauce
½ teaspoon vanilla
¾ cup dried cranberries
1 recipe Lemon Frosting (page 158)

Preheat the oven to 400 degrees. Lightly grease a 9 x 11-inch pan with margarine or oil, or line it with parchment paper.

In a medium bowl, whisk together flour, oatmeal, baking powder, cinnamon and salt. In a large bowl, cream together sugar and margarine. Add applesauce and vanilla. Add dry ingredients to wet ingredients in two batches. Stir in cranberries and combine until mixed through.

Spread batter in the bottom of the prepared pan and bake for 30 to 35 minutes, until lightly browned and a toothpick inserted into the center comes out clean. Let cool completely in the pan on a cooling rack before frosting with Lemon Frosting. Store bars covered at room temperature.

Yield: 20 BARS
Prep time: 30 MINUTES
Difficultly: 🥄🥄

LIME COCONUT BARS

I went through a citrus kick a while ago, and I just couldn't stop baking with it! These bars balance the sour limes with rich coconut milk and the crunchy crust with the creamy filling.

BASE:

½ cup margarine, melted

⅓ cup sugar

1 cup flour

1 cup quick oats

FILLING:

⅔ cup sugar

2 tablespoons cornstarch

pinch of salt

⅔ cup low-fat coconut milk

⅓ cup water

1 tablespoon lime zest

juice of 2 limes

⅓ cup toasted coconut (optional)

. . . .

Toast coconut in your oven or a toaster oven by sprinkling it on a clean pan and baking it at 350 degrees, stirring every 30 to 45 seconds, until golden.

. . . .

Instead of lime-coconut filling, top the base with the filling from Lemon Almond Torte (page 111) to make Lemon Bars!

Preheat the oven to 350 degrees. Lightly grease the bottom of an 8 x 8-inch pan with margarine or oil, or line it with parchment paper.

For Base: In a large bowl, combine melted margarine and sugar. Add flour to combine, then add oats. Press mixture into the bottom of the prepared pan, creating a lip around the edges, and bake for 10 to 15 minutes or until slightly browned.

For Filling: While crust is baking, combine sugar, cornstarch and salt in a medium saucepan or pot. Stir until well-combined. Add coconut milk and water and cook, stirring constantly, over medium heat until boiling, about 10 minutes. Add lime zest and juice and continue stirring until mixture is thick and bubbling. Pour into a separate bowl to let cool completely, stirring every few minutes.

Once lime mixture is cooled, pour into oatmeal shell and sprinkle with toasted coconut, if using. Let bars set in fridge for at least 2 hours before cutting. Store bars covered in the fridge.

Yield: 16 BARS

Prep time: 50 MINUTES

Difficulty:

MOCHA-DAMIA BARS

These bars are all grown-up! Mixing the instant coffee with the wet ingredients gives it time to start breaking down a bit and gives these bars a subtle kick. If you use salted macadamia nuts, omit the salt in the recipe.

2 cups flour

1 teaspoon baking soda

½ teaspoon salt

1 cup margarine, softened

½ cup brown sugar

½ cup sugar

¼ cup plain or vanilla yogurt

2 tablespoons instant coffee (you can add more or less, depending on your tastes)

1 teaspoon vanilla

½ cup chocolate chips

½ cup chopped macadamia nuts

Preheat the oven to 375 degrees. Lightly grease a 9 x 13-inch pan with margarine or oil, or line it with parchment paper.

In a medium bowl, mix together flour, baking soda and salt. In a large bowl, cream together margarine and sugar using an electric hand mixer. Add yogurt, coffee and vanilla and mix until well-combined. Add dry ingredients to wet ingredients in two batches and mix until batter is smooth; you may need to switch to using a spatula. Spread batter evenly into the prepared pan.

Bake 30 to 35 minutes, until edges are golden brown or a toothpick inserted into the center comes out clean. Let cool in the pan on a cooling rack for at least 45 minutes before cutting. Store bars covered at room temperature.

Yield: 15 BARS
Prep time: 30 MINUTES
Difficulty:

PEANUT BUTTER AND JELLY BARS

These bars will make you think you're back in elementary school and your friend with the warm bologna sandwich is trying to sweet-talk a trade with you. Think again! Concord grape jelly is perfect for the authentic, nostalgic taste, but you can make these bars a little more grown-up with some jam or preserves.

2 cups flour
¾ cup sugar
1 teaspoon baking powder
¼ teaspoon salt
¼ cup oil
½ cup peanut butter
¾ cup milk
⅔ cup grape jelly

Preheat the oven to 375 degrees. Lightly grease an 8 × 8-inch pan with margarine or oil, or line it with parchment paper.

In a medium bowl, mix together flour, sugar, baking powder and salt. In a large bowl, whisk together oil, peanut butter and milk. Add dry ingredients to wet ingredients in batches until just mixed. Reserve ¾ cup of dough and spread the rest in the bottom of the prepared pan.

Bake base for 20 minutes. Remove the pan from the oven and spread jelly on top of base. Crumble remaining topping over jelly and return the pan to the oven for 15 to 20 minutes until topping is browned and edges are set. Remove from the oven and let cool completely in the pan on a cooling rack before cutting into bars. Store bars covered at room temperature.

Yield: 12 BARS
Prep time: 25 MINUTES
Difficulty: 🥄🥄

Oatmeal Earth Bars

These chewy bars use cooked oatmeal to give them moisture and a delicious texture. They make a great snack and are a perfect way to use up leftover oatmeal.

1 ½ cups flour
½ teaspoon baking powder
¼ teaspoon salt
½ teaspoon cinnamon
¾ cup sugar
¾ cup applesauce
¼ cup oil
1 cup cooked oatmeal (traditional or steel-cut)
½ cup dried cherries
½ cup pecans, chopped

. . . .

This is a great recipe to mix up the add-ins. Try chocolate chips or chopped almonds for a different texture and taste!

Preheat the oven to 350 degrees. Lightly grease an 8 × 8-inch baking pan with margarine or oil, or line it with parchment paper.

In a medium bowl, combine flour, baking powder, salt and cinnamon. In a medium bowl, combine sugar and applesauce until mixed. Whisk in oil. Add cooked oatmeal and mix until well-incorporated. Add dry ingredients to wet ingredients in batches until just combined, then stir in cherries and pecans.

Spread batter into the prepared pan and bake for 40 to 45 minutes or until a toothpick inserted into the center comes out clean. The middle of the pan should feel set and the edges should be lightly browned. Let bars cool completely in the pan on a cooling rack before cutting. Store bars covered at room temperature.

Yield: 9 BARS
Prep time: 20 MINUTES
Difficulty:

NUTS FOR CAROB BARS

If you've been scared off by carob before, give it a try here. Try not to think of it as a chocolate substitute, because it's truly not. It's delicious in its own right and has a unique flavor. The carob lends a caramel taste to these bars and combines deliciously with the bananas, nuts and raisins.

1½ cups flour

⅓ cup carob powder

¼ teaspoon salt

1 teaspoon baking powder

2 large ripe bananas, mashed

¼ cup brown sugar, packed

¼ cup oil

1 teaspoon vanilla

⅔ cup milk

½ cup chocolate (or carob) chips

¼ cup nuts
(such as walnuts or pecans)

½ cup raisins

. . . .

Dried cranberries or chopped dried apricots are great substitutes for raisins in this recipe.

Preheat the oven to 350 degrees. Grease an 8 x 8-inch pan with margarine or oil, or line it with parchment paper.

In a small bowl, sift together flour, carob powder, salt and baking powder. In a large bowl, mix mashed banana, brown sugar, oil and vanilla until well-combined. Add milk. Add dry ingredients to wet ingredients in two batches. Stir in chocolate chips, nuts and raisins until just mixed. Spread mixture into the prepared pan and bake for 30 to 35 minutes or until toothpick inserted into the center comes out clean. Store bars covered at room temperature.

Yield: 9 BARS
Prep time: 30 MINUTES
Difficulty: 🥄 🥄

APRICOT BARS

I absolutely love apricots and you will, too, after trying these buttery bars. The mixture of the firm base, tart preserves and crumbly topping are sure to please your taste buds.

BASE:

½ cup margarine, softened

½ cup sugar

1¼ cups flour

¼ teaspoon salt

TOPPING:

⅓ cup plus 1 tablespoon flour

¼ cup sugar

3 tablespoons margarine, chilled

1¼ cups apricot preserves

Preheat the oven to 350 degrees. Lightly grease an 8 × 8-inch pan with margarine or oil, or line it with parchment paper.

For Base: In a medium bowl, cream together margarine and sugar. In a small bowl, mix flour and salt. Add dry ingredients to wet ingredients in batches to make a stiff dough. Spread dough in the bottom of the prepared pan and poke several times with the tines of a fork to make air holes. Bake for 20 minutes.

For Topping: While base is baking, mix together flour and sugar. Cut in margarine with the back of a fork or pastry cutter until mixture is coarse and crumbly. Keep topping in fridge to keep margarine cool after mixing. After base has baked for 20 minutes, spread preserves over the top and sprinkle topping on.

Return the pan to the oven for 20 to 25 minutes or until topping is browned. Remove from the oven and let cool on a cooling rack for 30 minutes before cutting. Store bars covered at room temperature.

Yield: 12 BARS

Prep time: 30 MINUTES

Difficulty:

FUDGY MACAROON BARS

Macaroons usually come in one of two varieties: almond or coconut. These bars combine the two for a moist bar with a soft and delicious texture. The almonds add a toothsome touch to the coconut. The Fudgy Frosting takes the whole thing over the edge.

2½ cups sweetened shredded coconut

½ cup almond meal or ground almonds

½ cup flour

⅓ cup sugar

⅓ cup applesauce

⅔ cup milk

1 tablespoon melted margarine

1 recipe Fudgy Frosting (page 157)

. . . .

If you can't find almond meal, you can easily grind up slivered almonds in a food processor.

Preheat the oven to 350 degrees. Lightly grease an 8 x 8-inch pan with margarine or oil, or line it with parchment paper.

In a large bowl, mix coconut, almonds, flour and sugar until well-combined. Make a well in the middle of the mixture and add applesauce, milk and margarine. Stir until batter is just combined and all of coconut mixture is moist.

Spread batter into the prepared pan. Bake for 35 to 38 minutes or until lightly browned and center is set. Let cool completely on a cooling rack before frosting with a batch of Fudgy Frosting. Store bars covered in fridge.

Yield: 16 BARS
Prep time: 25 MINUTES
Difficulty:

MUFFINS

Muffins are my favorite breakfast treat. I usually make jumbo-sized muffins because they are the perfect size for a whole meal. They are quick to make and you can incorporate lots of nutritious add-ins such as nuts or dried fruit. It's not all about nuts and berries, though, and I am not immune to decadent muffins. Some muffins are like dessert for breakfast!

If you use muffin-tin liners, your muffins will be softer than if you grease the tins, but either way, you'll be sure to have a fistful of deliciousness in the end.

- BLUEBERRY STREUSEL MUFFINS
- ORANGE CHOCOLATE MUFFINS
- LESLIE'S AWESOMENESS MUFFINS
- FRENCH TOAST MUFFINS
- GARDEN MUFFINS
- CHOCOLATE RASPBERRY SWIRL MUFFINS
- RANDY'S UPSIDE-DOWN STICKY MUFFINS
- PEARY BERRY MUFFINS
- LEMON ALMOND BLING MUFFINS
- EGGNOG MUFFINS WITH BOOZY RAISINS
- RASPBERRY LIME MUFFINS

BLUEBERRY STREUSEL MUFFINS

When Jim and I were first married, I asked him what his favorite muffin was and he loved these muffins that came from a boxed mix with a little can of blueberries. Yuck! I knew I could do better than that. These are the ultimate breakfast muffin. If you're not keen on blueberries, try different kinds of berries, like blackberries or cherries.

BATTER:

2¼ cups plus 2 tablespoons flour, divided

¾ cup sugar

1 tablespoon baking powder

⅛ teaspoon salt

1¼ cups milk

¼ plus 2 tablespoons oil

½ cup plus 2 tablespoons yogurt (equal to 1 6-ounce container)

½ teaspoon vanilla

1¼ cups fresh or frozen blueberries (not thawed)

TOPPING:

¼ cup flour

2 tablespoons sugar

2 tablespoons cold margarine

Preheat the oven to 400 degrees. Lightly grease 12 regular or 6 jumbo muffin cups with margarine or oil, or line with paper liners.

For Batter: In a large bowl, combine 2¼ cups flour, sugar, baking powder and salt. In a medium bowl, combine milk, oil, yogurt and vanilla. In another bowl, toss blueberries with remaining 2 tablespoons flour. Add wet ingredients to dry ingredients and mix until just incorporated. Add blueberries and gently combine.

For Topping: In a small bowl, mix flour and sugar and cut in margarine with a pastry cutter or with your fingers until mixture is crumbly.

Spoon batter into muffin tin, filling each cup until almost full. Evenly sprinkle topping on each muffin. Bake for 15 to 20 minutes for regular muffins or 20 to 25 minutes for jumbo, until muffins are golden and a toothpick comes out clean. Cool for 10 minutes in the pan and then transfer to a cooling rack and let cool completely. Store leftover muffins covered at room temperature.

Yield: 12 REGULAR OR 6 JUMBO MUFFINS
Prep time: 30 MINUTES
Difficulty:

ORANGE CHOCOLATE MUFFINS

I didn't really learn to appreciate the combination of orange and chocolate until I became an adult, but now it rules the roost! The moist texture of this fluffy muffin with a boost of orange zest is perfectly accented by the chocolate chips scattered throughout. Nom, nom, nom!

2¼ cups flour

¾ cup sugar

1 teaspoon baking powder

1 teaspoon baking soda

⅛ teaspoon salt

1⅔ cups milk

⅓ cup oil

zest of one large orange

juice of one large orange

½ teaspoon vanilla

½ cup chocolate chips

Preheat the oven to 350 degrees. Lightly grease 12 regular or 6 jumbo muffin cups, or line with paper liners.

In a medium bowl, combine flour, sugar, baking powder, baking soda and salt. In a large bowl, combine milk, oil, orange zest, orange juice and vanilla. Add dry ingredients to wet ingredients in two batches until just mixed. Stir in chocolate chips.

Spoon batter into muffin tin, filling each cup until almost full. Bake for 18 to 20 minutes for regular muffins or 25 to 30 minutes for jumbo, until muffins are lightly golden and a toothpick comes out clean. Remove from the oven and let cool completely before removing from the tin. Store leftover muffins covered at room temperature.

Yield: 12 REGULAR OR 6 JUMBO MUFFINS
Prep time: 25 MINUTES
Difficulty:

LESLIE'S AWESOMENESS MUFFINS

My friend Leslie loves dates and nuts and, well, everything that tastes good, really! We're both sweet-a-holics so when I developed these muffins, I thought of her because they are very low in sugar but still have enough sweetness to satisfy. They definitely get her approval for being full of "awesomeness."

1¼ cups white whole-wheat flour (or all-purpose flour)

2 teaspoons baking powder

½ teaspoon baking soda

½ teaspoon cinnamon

⅛ teaspoon salt

1 cup mashed ripe banana (approximately 2 medium bananas)

½ cup milk

¼ cup oil

2 tablespoons blackstrap molasses

2 tablespoons maple syrup

1 cup old-fashioned oats

1 cup chopped dates

½ cup chopped nuts

. . . .

If you don't have any bananas around, or just don't like them, substitute with applesauce.

Preheat the oven to 375 degrees. Lightly grease 12 regular or 6 jumbo muffin cups with margarine or oil, or line with paper liners.

In a large bowl, combine flour, baking powder, baking soda, cinnamon and salt. In a separate bowl, mix together banana, milk, oil, molasses and maple syrup until combined. Add oatmeal and let sit to moisten oats. Add wet ingredients to dry ingredients and mix until just combined. Gently mix in dates and nuts.

Spoon batter into muffin tin, filling each up almost to the top. Bake for 15 to 17 minutes for regular-sized muffins or 22 to 27 minutes for jumbo, until muffins are golden and a toothpick comes out clean. Cool in the muffin tin on a cooling rack for 15 minutes, then transfer muffins directly onto the rack to finish cooling. Store leftover muffins covered at room temperature.

Yield: 12 REGULAR OR 6 JUMBO MUFFINS

Prep time: 25 MINUTES

Difficulty:

French Toast Muffins

It used to seem unfortunate that french toast couldn't be more portable and less time consuming, because it's so darn tasty. Well, now you can make these muffins and you'll always have french toast on the go!

2¼ cups flour

¾ cup sugar

2 teaspoons baking powder

⅛ teaspoon salt

1 teaspoon cinnamon

1¼ cups milk

⅓ cup oil

½ cup plus 2 tablespoons yogurt (equivalent to 1 6-ounce container)

1½ teaspoons maple extract

½ teaspoon vanilla

cinnamon and powered sugar, for topping

. . . .

For extra maple goodness, combine 1 tablespoon maple syrup with ½ cup sifted powdered sugar and glaze the tops of the muffins with the maple topping before sifting on the cinnamon and powdered sugar.

Preheat the oven to 350 degrees. Lightly grease 12 regular or 6 jumbo muffin cups with margarine or oil, or line with paper liners.

In a medium bowl, combine flour, sugar, baking powder, salt and cinnamon. In a large bowl, mix together milk, oil, yogurt, maple extract and vanilla. Add dry ingredients to wet ingredients in two batches until just mixed.

Spoon batter into muffin tin, filling each cup until almost full. Bake for 18 to 20 minutes for regular muffins or 25 to 30 minutes for jumbo, until muffins are lightly golden and a toothpick comes out clean. Remove muffins from the oven and let cool completely before removing from the tin and transferring to a cooling rack. Sift powdered sugar and cinnamon on top of each muffin. Store leftover muffins covered at room temperature.

Yield: 12 REGULAR OR 6 JUMBO MUFFINS
Prep time: 25 MINUTES
Difficulty: 🥄

GARDEN MUFFINS

I love to eat these muffins slightly warm with a melty pat of margarine in the middle. They are full of veggies and whole-grain goodness and are the perfect way to get some nutrition into lazy or picky eaters.

1½ cups white-wheat flour (or all-purpose flour)

½ cup oat bran (or ½ cup slightly ground instant oats)

2 teaspoons baking powder

¼ teaspoon salt

1 teaspoon cinnamon

½ cup unsweetened applesauce

¼ cup maple syrup or agave nectar

¼ cup oil

1 cup grated zucchini

½ cup grated carrots

¾ cup milk

½ cup raisins (optional)

¼ cup walnuts (optional)

. . . .

Out of maple syrup or agave? You can still make these muffins by subbing ¼ cup of sugar.

Preheat the oven to 375 degrees. Lightly grease 12 regular or 6 jumbo muffin cups with margarine or oil, or line with paper liners.

In a large bowl, combine flour, oat bran, baking powder, salt and cinnamon. In another large bowl, combine applesauce, maple syrup and oil. Add zucchini and carrots and then stir in milk. Add wet ingredients to dry ingredients, then stir in raisins and walnuts and mix until well-combined.

Spoon batter into muffin tin, filling each cup until almost full and bake for 18 to 20 minutes for regular muffins or 25 to 30 minutes for jumbo, until muffins are lightly golden and toothpick comes out clean. Let muffins cool in the pan for 5 minutes, then transfer to finish cooling on a cooling rack. Store leftover muffins covered at room temperature.

Yield: 12 REGULAR OR 6 JUMBO MUFFFINS
Prep time: 30 MINUTES
Difficulty: ✎ ✎

CHOCOLATE RASPBERRY SWIRL MUFFINS

Sometimes you just need something decadent for a snack or dessert (or if you're like me, upon waking). When you're in need of a chocolate fix, these muffins will provide you with the support that you need to get out of bed and lay around on your couch, surrounded by muffin liners.

1¾ cups flour

⅓ cup baking cocoa, sifted

½ teaspoon baking powder

½ teaspoon baking soda

¼ teaspoon salt

⅓ cup oil

½ cup sugar

1 cup milk

½ cup plus 2 tablespoons yogurt (equal to 1 6-ounce container)

1 teaspoon vanilla

¼ cup roughly chopped chocolate

½ cup raspberry preserves

. . . .

For these muffins it's best to do your toothpick test at an angle, from the edge of the muffin, so you poke below the swirl.

Preheat the oven to 350 degrees. Lightly grease 12 regular or 6 jumbo muffin cups with margarine or oil, or line with paper liners.

In a large bowl, whisk together flour, baking cocoa, baking powder, baking soda and salt. In a medium bowl, combine oil and sugar. Add milk, yogurt and vanilla and mix until creamy. Add wet ingredients to dry ingredients until just combined, then stir in chocolate.

Spoon batter into muffin tins, filling each cup almost to the top. Spoon preserves on top of each muffin, using ½ teaspoon for each regular muffin or 1 teaspoon for each jumbo muffin. Swirl preserves into muffins using a toothpick or a butter knife.

Bake for 19 to 22 minutes for regular muffins or 28 to 32 minutes for jumbo, until middles of muffin tops look set and a toothpick comes out clean (some preserves may stick). Let muffins cool in the tin for 10 minutes, then transfer to a cooling rack to cool completely. Store leftover muffins covered at room temperature.

Yield: 12 REGULAR OR 6 JUMBO MUFFINS
Prep time: 35 MINUTES
Difficulty: 🥄🥄🥄

Randy's Upside-Down Sticky Muffins

Gooey pecan sticky buns were favorite morning pastries of my father, Randy. On the occasion that we had them in the house, he had to race me to eat them. Regular sticky buns can be a serious production to make due to all of the steps involved. Here, these easy muffins have a simple gooey topping that makes them an irresistible treat that will have you running to the kitchen!

TOPPING:

¼ cup corn syrup or brown rice syrup

2 tablespoons margarine

½ cup brown sugar

BATTER:

2 cups flour

1 cup sugar

2 teaspoons baking powder

1 teaspoon cinnamon

¼ teaspoon salt

1 cup milk

⅓ cup oil

½ cup plus 2 tablespoons yogurt (equivalent of 1 6-ounce container)

1 teaspoon vanilla

1 cup chopped pecans

For Topping: In a small saucepan, combine corn syrup or brown rice syrup, margarine and brown sugar. Heat on medium until margarine is melted and all ingredients are incorporated, stirring frequently. Remove from heat and set aside to cool slightly while you prepare the muffin batter.

Preheat the oven to 350 degrees. Grease the sides of 12 regular muffin cups or 6 jumbo muffin cups and line the cup bottoms with parchment paper or waxed paper circles. If you do not have parchment paper or waxed paper, grease the bottoms well so the topping will come out easily when you flip the pan over.

For Batter: In a small bowl, combine flour, sugar, baking powder, cinnamon and salt. In a medium bowl, combine milk, oil, yogurt and vanilla until well-mixed. Add dry ingredients to wet ingredients in batches until just incorporated. Do not overmix.

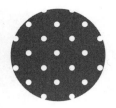

For Assembly: Divide prepared brown sugar syrup and pecans equally among the bottoms of the muffin cups. Spoon the muffin batter on top of the syrup and pecans, filling each cup almost to the top. Bake 18 to 20 minutes for regular muffins or 25 to 30 for jumbo muffins, until a toothpick comes out clean. Immediately invert onto a baking sheet lined with waxed paper and remove muffin tin so the pecan caramel can ooze down the sides of the muffins. Remove parchment paper or waxed paper circles. If you did not use parchment paper in the bottoms, you may need to spoon the pecans back onto the muffins. Store leftover muffins covered at room temperature.

Yield: 12 REGULAR OR 6 JUMBO MUFFINS
Prep time: 35 MINUTES
Difficulty:

PEARY BERRY MUFFINS

These muffins make good use of lingering pears during those fall and winter months when they are plentiful. You can use pears that are a little too firm for eating, as the stone of the fruit adds a nice texture to these muffins.

2¼ cups flour

¾ cup sugar

2 teaspoons baking powder

⅛ teaspoon salt

¼ cup oil

½ teaspoon vanilla

½ teaspoon mild vinegar

1 cup milk

2 medium pears, peeled and shredded

1 cup mixed berries, fresh or frozen

Preheat the oven to 400 degrees. Lightly grease 12 regular or 6 jumbo muffin cups with margarine or oil, or line with paper liners.

In a large bowl, combine flour, sugar, baking powder and salt. In a medium bowl, combine oil, vanilla, vinegar and milk. Add pears and mix to combine. Incorporate wet ingredients into dry ingredients until just mixed, then gently fold in berries.

Spoon batter into the muffin tin, filling each cup almost to the top. Bake for 20 to 25 minutes for regular-sized muffins or 28 to 30 minutes for jumbo, until golden and a toothpick comes out clean. Let cool in the tin for 15 minutes, then remove from the tin to cool on a cooling rack. Store leftover muffins covered at room temperature.

Yield: 12 REGULAR OR 6 JUMBO MUFFINS
Prep time: 25 MINUTES
Difficulty:

Lemon Almond Bling Muffins

These muffins are more about the flavor of almonds than the texture of them. I love the topping because it gives the muffins character, and the hint of almonds and lemon zest add the perfect crunch to this subtle flavor combination.

BATTER:

2¼ cups flour

¾ cup sugar

2 teaspoons baking powder

⅛ teaspoon salt

1¼ cups milk

⅓ cup oil

½ cup plus 2 tablespoons yogurt (equal to 1 6-ounce container)

1 teaspoon almond extract (optional)

2 teaspoons lemon juice

TOPPING:

¼ cup sugar

zest of one lemon (about 2 teaspoons)

¼ cup sliced almonds

Preheat the oven to 400 degrees. Lightly grease 12 regular or 6 jumbo muffin cups with margarine or oil, or line with paper liners.

For Batter: In a large bowl, combine flour, sugar, baking powder and salt. In a medium bowl, combine milk, oil, yogurt, almond extract and lemon juice. Add wet ingredients to dry ingredients and combine until just mixed.

For Topping: In a small bowl, mix topping sugar, lemon zest and sliced almonds.

Spoon batter into the muffin tin, filling each cup almost to the top. Sprinkle on topping. Bake for 15 to 17 minutes for regular muffins or 22 to 25 minutes for jumbo, until the muffins are golden and a toothpick comes out clean. Cool for 10 minutes in the pan and then transfer to a cooling rack to finish cooling. Store leftover muffins covered at room temperature.

Yield: 12 REGULAR OR 6 JUMBO MUFFINS
Prep time: 25 MINUTES
Difficulty:

Eggnog Muffins with Boozy Raisins

These muffins are the holiday season in a muffin liner, spiced and spiked with festive deliciousness. For all of the eggnog lovers in your life, these are sure to be a hit. If you prefer a different booze in your eggnog, feel free to substitute.

⅓ cup raisins

⅓ cup rum, warmed

2¼ cups flour

¾ cup sugar

2 teaspoons baking powder

¼ teaspoon salt

½ teaspoon cinnamon

¼ teaspoon nutmeg

1½ cups eggnog
(rice or soy are both fine)

⅓ cup oil

½ cup plus 2 tablespoons yogurt
(equal to 1 6-ounce container)

½ teaspoon vanilla

¾ cup powdered sugar

• •

The alcohol in this recipe is optional and can be replaced with warm water.

Preheat the oven to 400 degrees. Lightly grease 12 regular or 6 jumbo muffin cups with margarine or oil, or line with paper liners.

In a small bowl, combine raisins and rum. Let sit for a few minutes to plump raisins. In a large bowl, combine flour, sugar, baking powder, salt, cinnamon and nutmeg. In a medium bowl, whisk together eggnog, oil, yogurt and vanilla. Add wet ingredients to dry ingredients and mix until just moistened. Reserve 1 tablespoon rum and drain remaining rum from raisins. Gently mix raisins into muffin batter.

Spoon batter into the muffin tin, filling each cup almost to the top. Bake for 15 to 18 minutes for regular muffins and 25 to 28 minutes for jumbo, until muffins are lightly golden and a toothpick comes out clean. Let cool completely in muffin tin on a cooling rack.

In a small bowl, combine reserved tablespoon of rum with powdered sugar. Lightly brush glaze onto tops of cooled muffins. Sprinkle with cinnamon or nutmeg if desired. Store leftover muffins covered at room temperature.

Yield: 12 REGULAR OR 6 JUMBO MUFFINS
Prep time: 25 MINUTES
Difficulty:

RASPBERRY LIME MUFFINS

Raspberry and lime make a great flavor combination, especially if you are fond of slightly tart baked goods. If you use frozen raspberries, be sure they aren't completely thawed and don't overmix the batter or you'll have blue, streaky muffins!

1 cup white whole-wheat flour
(or all-purpose flour)

1 cup all-purpose flour

2 teaspoons baking powder

¼ teaspoon salt

¾ cup granulated sugar

¼ cup oil

1 cup plus 2 tablespoons milk

1 teaspoon vanilla

zest of one lime

juice of one lime

1½ cups raspberries
(fresh or frozen)

Preheat the oven to 350 degrees. Lightly grease 12 regular or 6 jumbo muffin cups with margarine or oil, or line with paper liners.

In a medium bowl, sift together whole-wheat flour, all-purpose flour, baking powder and salt. In a large bowl, mix sugar and oil. Add milk, vanilla and lime zest and juice. Add dry ingredients to wet ingredients and combine until just mixed, then gently fold in raspberries.

Spoon batter into muffin tin, filling each up almost to the top. Bake for 16 to 19 minutes for regular muffins or 22 to 26 minutes for jumbo, until muffins are golden and a toothpick comes out clean. Let cool in the tin for 10 minutes, then transfer to a cooling rack. Store leftover muffins covered at room temperature.

Yield: 12 REGULAR OR 6 JUMBO MUFFINS
Prep time: 25 MINUTES
Difficulty:

QUICK BREADS

Quick breads are wonderful because they provide a quick side dish to eat with soup or chili or can be a slice of warmth and sweetness on a cold morning. They don't require the prep and extra attention that yeasted breads do; you can basically dump the ingredients into a loaf pan and you're done. Simple yet impressive, just the way I like it.

- BEST BANANA BREAD
- YOU ARE MY SUNSHINE LOAF
- CORNIN' AROUND BREAD
- GOING, GOING, GONE! GINGERBREAD
- CHOCOLATE STOUT BREAD
- SWEET POTATO BREAD
- BAKLAVA BREAD
- PUMPKIN CINN-A-ZAG BREAD
- SAUCY APPLE BREAD
- IRISH SODA BREAD
- BASIC BISCUITS
- BETTAH CHETTAH BISCUITS

BEST BANANA BREAD

I have been told by multiple people that this is the best banana bread they have ever had, vegan or otherwise. After hearing this several times, I had to have my co-worker, who is a banana bread connoisseur, weigh in with his opinion and he agreed. Success! Try adding walnuts or pecans to this bread for a textural treat. Don't like "stuff" in your bread? Eat it as is.

1 ½ cups flour

2 teaspoons baking powder

½ teaspoon baking soda

¼ teaspoon salt

⅓ cup oil

½ cup brown sugar, packed

1 cup mashed banana
(about 2 bananas)

⅓ cup milk

Preheat the oven to 350 degrees. Lightly grease a 9 × 5-inch loaf pan with margarine or oil.

In a small bowl, combine flour, baking powder, baking soda and salt. In a large bowl, combine oil and brown sugar. Add bananas and milk and stir to combine. Add dry ingredients to wet ingredients and mix until just combined.

Spread batter in the loaf pan and bake for 43 to 48 minutes, until bread is golden and a toothpick comes out clean. Let cool in the pan for 30 minutes. Run a knife around the edge to loosen, and turn bread out of the pan to let cool on a cooling rack. Store leftover bread covered at room temperature.

Yield: 1 LOAF, 10 SLICES
Prep time: 25 MINUTES
Difficulty:

YOU ARE MY SUNSHINE LOAF

This bread is so bright and sunny you can almost feel the sunshine on your face. If California could be made in the form of a bread, this would be it. With its lovely orange color and citrus notes, along with sweet bursts of raisins, this is a welcome breakfast bread on the grayest days of winter.

1 ½ cups all-purpose flour

1 cup white-wheat flour (or all-purpose flour)

½ cup sugar

2 teaspoons baking powder

¼ teaspoon salt

1 cup shredded carrots

1 medium apple, peeled and shredded

1 ½ cups milk

¼ cup oil

zest of 1 medium orange

juice of one medium orange

½ cup raisins

½ cup walnuts

Preheat the oven to 350 degrees. Lightly grease a 9 × 5-inch loaf pan with margarine or oil.

In a medium bowl, combine all-purpose flour, white-wheat flour, sugar, baking powder and salt. In a large bowl, combine shredded carrots, shredded apple and milk and mix until well-combined. Add oil, orange zest and orange juice. Add dry ingredients to wet ingredients in two batches until just combined. Gently mix in raisins and walnuts.

Spread batter in the loaf pan and bake for 50 to 55 minutes, until bread is golden and a toothpick comes out clean. Let cool in the pan on a cooling rack until the pan is cool enough to touch, about 40 minutes. Run a knife around the outside of the loaf to separate it from the pan, and turn bread out of the pan to finish cooling on a rack. Store leftover bread covered at room temperature

Yield: 1 LOAF, 10 SLICES

Prep time: 30 MINUTES

Difficulty:

CORNIN' AROUND BREAD

Mmm, cornbread. This slightly sweet bread is perfect crumbled over chili or soup. It's easy enough to whip up while your meal is simmering. You can make this in muffin cups if you'd like, or you can add a little chili pepper for a southwest flair. Try to buy organic cornmeal if you can; you don't want any mutant GMO corn bread in your kitchen!

1 cup flour
1 cup cornmeal
⅓ cup sugar
2 teaspoons baking powder
¼ teaspoon salt
¼ cup unsweetened applesauce
⅓ cup oil
1 cup milk
¼ cup frozen sweet corn

Preheat the oven to 400 degrees. Lightly grease an 8 x 8-inch baking pan with margarine or oil.

In a large bowl, whisk together flour, cornmeal, sugar, baking powder and salt. In another bowl, mix applesauce with oil, then whisk in milk. Add wet ingredients to dry ingredients and mix until just combined, then stir in corn.

Spread batter into the pan and bake for 30 to 35 minutes, until bread is lightly browned and a toothpick comes out clean. Store leftover bread covered at room temperature.

Yield: 9 SQUARES
Prep time: 20 MINUTES
Difficulty:

GOING, GOING, GONE! GINGERBREAD

When it's rainy and gray in Portland, it's easy to forget that it's wintertime, and feeling the joy of the holiday season can be a stretch. The easiest, and tastiest, way to remedy this is by whipping up a batch of gingerbread. This bread is moist and sweet and spiked with just the right amount of spice. Even Jim, who insists that he doesn't like gingerbread, devours this fragrant loaf.

2 cups flour

2 teaspoons ground ginger

1 teaspoon cinnamon

1 teaspoon baking soda

1 teaspoon baking powder

¼ teaspoon nutmeg

¼ teaspoon salt

1 cup milk

½ cup oil

1 cup plus 1 tablespoon sugar, divided

¼ cup molasses

1 teaspoon vinegar

1 teaspoon fresh grated ginger (optional)

. . . .

Try adding ¼ cup chopped candied ginger to this bread for some added kick and texture.

Preheat the oven to 350 degrees. If you want a gingerbread loaf, lightly grease a 9 × 5-inch loaf pan. If you prefer to have gingerbread squares, lightly grease an 8 × 8-inch baking dish.

In a large bowl, combine flour, ground ginger, cinnamon, baking soda, baking powder, nutmeg and salt. In a medium bowl, combine oil and 1 cup sugar. Whisk in molasses until mixture is smooth. Add milk and vinegar and whisk until well-combined, then add fresh ginger, if using. Add wet ingredients to dry ingredients and mix until just moistened, making sure that there are no pockets of the dry ingredients remaining.

Spread batter into the prepared pan and sprinkle with remaining 1 tablespoon sugar. For a gingerbread loaf, bake for 55 to 60 minutes or until a toothpick comes out clean. For gingerbread squares, bake for 40 to 45 minutes or until a toothpick comes out clean. Let cool in the pan on a cooling rack completely before serving. Store leftover bread covered at room temperature.

Yield: 10 SLICES OR 16 SQUARES
Prep time: 30 MINUTES
Difficulty:

CHOCOLATE STOUT BREAD

This bread is a little more grown-up than some of the other recipes. It is a bit more savory, with a hint of chocolate and that fermented edge from the stout. This bread is a fantastic snack with your favorite bottle of beer on a hot summer afternoon.

2¾ cups flour
⅓ cup baking cocoa, sifted
1 cup sugar
2 teaspoons baking powder
¼ teaspoon salt
1½ cups chocolate stout
¼ cup oil
⅓ cup milk

Preheat the oven to 350 degrees. Lightly grease a 9 x 5-inch loaf pan with margarine or oil.

In a large bowl, combine flour, cocoa, sugar, baking powder and salt. Make a well in the middle of dry ingredients and add stout, oil and milk. Mix until just combined.

Spread batter into the loaf pan and bake for 45 to 50 minutes or until a toothpick comes out clean. Let loaf cool in the pan for 30 minutes before turning out on a cooling rack to finish cooling. Store leftover bread covered at room temperature.

Yield: 1 LOAF, 10 SLICES
Prep time: 25 MINUTES
Difficulty: 🥄

SWEET POTATO BREAD

This fragrant, moist bread is sweet enough to enjoy as a treat but savory enough to eat with a bowl of soup. Feel free to use canned or freshly puréed sweet potatoes, or try yams.

1 ½ cups flour

2 teaspoons baking powder

¼ teaspoon salt

1 teaspoon cinnamon

½ cup brown sugar

½ cup orange juice

½ cup applesauce

¼ cup oil

⅓ cup milk

1 cup sweet potato purée

½ cup chopped pecans (optional)

Preheat the oven to 325 degrees. Lightly grease a 9 × 5-inch loaf pan with margarine or oil.

In a large bowl, combine flour, baking powder, salt and cinnamon. In a separate bowl, combine brown sugar, orange juice, applesauce, oil, milk and sweet potato purée until well-mixed (you may need to use an electric hand mixer on a low speed). Add wet ingredients to dry ingredients and mix well until the batter is just moistened. Stir in pecans, if using.

Spread batter into prepared pan. Bake for about 1 hour until loaf is lightly browned and a toothpick comes out clean. Cool in the pan on a cooling rack for 45 minutes. Run a knife around the edge to loosen and turn loaf out of the pan to finish cooling on the rack. Store leftover bread covered at room temperature.

Yield: 1 LOAF, 10 SLICES
Prep time: 25 MINUTES
Difficulty:

BAKLAVA BREAD

I love baklava, and while I like a baking challenge, making baklava from scratch is more of a challenge than I'm looking for. This bread will satisfy any craving you may have for Mediterranean sweets and will also make you question why we don't use pistachios more in American baking traditions.

BREAD:

3 cups flour

¼ cup sugar

1 teaspoon baking powder

1 teaspoon baking soda

1 teaspoon cinnamon

½ teaspoon salt

1⅓ cups milk

1 teaspoon mild vinegar

½ cup melted margarine

¾ cup plus 2 tablespoons pistachios, chopped, divided

SYRUP:

⅔ cup sugar

¼ cup agave nectar

¼ cup water

Preheat the oven to 350 degrees. Lightly grease a 9 × 5-inch loaf pan with margarine or oil.

For Bread: In a medium bowl, combine flour, sugar, baking powder, baking soda, cinnamon and salt. In a large bowl, combine milk and vinegar and let sit for 2 minutes. Add melted margarine and whisk to combine. Add dry ingredients to wet ingredients in batches until just mixed, then add ¾ cup pistachios.

Spread batter in the loaf pan and bake for 48 to 52 minutes or until a toothpick comes out clean. Remove from the oven and let cool in the pan on a cooling rack.

For Syrup: Combine sugar, agave nectar and water in a saucepan over medium heat. Stirring continuously, cook until sugar dissolves and syrup bubbles, about 7 to 10 minutes. Remove from heat and let cool.

Using a pointed object, such as a straw or a chopstick, poke 2-inch holes in top of loaf. Pour half of syrup over loaf and let sit until all syrup is absorbed, then pour on remaining syrup. After all syrup is absorbed, sprinkle bread with remaining 2 tablespoons of pistachios. Let loaf cool completely before serving. Store leftover bread covered at room temperature.

Yield: 1 LOAF, 10 SLICES
Prep time: 40 MINUTES
Difficulty:

PUMPKIN CINN-A-ZAG BREAD

This bread came from a combination of ideas submitted by readers on my blog. One person suggested pumpkin bread and another suggested cinnamon swirl. Several others wanted a bread without any nuts in it. This was the result!

1½ cups flour

¾ cup sugar

1½ teaspoons baking soda

2 tablespoons plus 1 teaspoon cinnamon

1 teaspoon pumpkin pie spice

½ teaspoon salt

1 cup pumpkin purée (not pumpkin pie mix)

¼ cup oil

¼ cup apple butter (or apple sauce)

½ cup milk

¼ cup brown sugar

. . . .

As with anything pumpkin, this bread is even better the next day, when the spices have had some time to really meld together.

Preheat the oven to 350 degrees. Lightly grease a 9 x 5-inch loaf pan with margarine or oil.

In a large bowl, combine flour, sugar, baking soda, 1 teaspoon cinnamon, pumpkin pie spice and salt. In a medium bowl, whisk together pumpkin, oil, apple butter and milk. Add wet ingredients to dry ingredients and stir until just mixed. In a small bowl, mix together brown sugar and 2 tablespoons cinnamon; set aside.

Pour half of batter into the loaf pan, then sprinkle with brown sugar mixture. Pour remaining batter on top. Draw a knife through the loaf in several directions to mix the zig-zag layer around.

Bake for 48 to 52 minutes until center of bread is set and a toothpick comes out clean. Let loaf cool in the pan on a cooling rack for 45 minutes. Run a knife around the edge to loosen and turn bread out of the pan to finish cooling on the rack. Store leftover bread covered at room temperature.

Yield: 1 LOAF, 10 SLICES
Prep time: 25 MINUTES
Difficulty: ✎ ✎

SAUCY APPLE BREAD

This moist bread is chock full of appley goodness. With its crunchy pecan topping, it is the perfect breakfast bread, lightly toasted with some melted margarine on top... I can taste it now.

BATTER:

2 cups flour

1 teaspoon baking powder

1 teaspoon baking soda

1 teaspoon cinnamon

¼ teaspoon salt

¾ cup sugar

⅓ cup oil

1 cup applesauce

¼ cup milk

1 medium apple, peeled and chopped

TOPPING:

¼ cup sugar

¼ cup flour

2 tablespoons cold margarine

⅓ cup chopped pecans

Preheat the oven to 350 degrees. Lightly grease a 9 × 5-inch loaf pan with margarine or oil.

For Batter: In a medium bowl, combine flour, baking powder, baking soda, cinnamon and salt. In a large bowl, combine sugar and oil. Add applesauce and milk and mix well. Incorporate dry ingredients into wet ingredients until just mixed. Stir in chopped apple.

For Topping: In a small bowl, combine sugar and flour. Cut in margarine with the back of a fork until mixture is crumbly. Add pecans.

Spread batter into the loaf pan and sprinkle topping on top of bread. Bake for 52 to 55 minutes, until topping is browned and a toothpick comes out clean. Let bread cool completely on a cooling rack before serving. Store leftover bread covered at room temperature.

Yield: 1 LOAF, 10 SLICES

Prep time: 30 MINUTES

Difficulty:

Irish Soda Bread

Irish Soda Bread is a lifesaver when you want to make a hearty meal but don't have the time to wait around for a loaf of bread to rise. It whips up in a cinch and relies on baking soda to quickly rise to the occasion (hence the "soda bread" part). You can make oat flour by processing dried oats (traditional, not steel-cut) in a food processor for a few spins until they are coarse and grainy.

1½ cups flour
½ cup oat flour
2 teaspoons baking soda
¼ teaspoon salt
1 cup milk
1 teaspoon mild vinegar

Preheat the oven to 400 degrees. Line a baking sheet with parchment paper.

In a medium bowl, mix flour, oat flour, baking soda and salt. In a small bowl, mix milk and vinegar together and let sit for 2 minutes. Create a well in the dry ingredients and pour wet ingredients in the middle. Mix until just incorporated, and shape dough into a ball. Dough may be a little floury on the outside and that is fine.

Place dough on the baking sheet and bake for 30 to 35 minutes or until bread is browned and sounds hollow when tapped. Let cool 15 minutes before serving. Store leftover bread covered at room temperature.

Yield: 1 LOAF, ABOUT 8 SLICES
Prep time: 20 MINUTES
Difficulty:

Basic Biscuits

Biscuits are a great standby when you don't have time to make bread or if you just want to have something warm and starchy to smother with gravy. Feel free to roll them out on a floured surface and cut them with a glass or biscuit cutter. Call me weird (or lazy), but I like mine blobby and irregular.

1 cup all-purpose flour
1 cup whole-wheat pastry flour
(or all-purpose flour)
2 teaspoons baking powder
1 teaspoon baking soda
¼ teaspoon salt
¾ cup milk
1 teaspoon mild vinegar
¼ cup oil

Preheat the oven to 425 degrees. Line a baking sheet with parchment paper.

In a large bowl, combine all-purpose flour, whole-wheat pastry flour, baking powder, baking soda and salt. In a medium bowl, mix milk and vinegar. Let sit for 2 minutes. Add oil and whisk quickly. Add wet ingredients to dry ingredients and mix until just combined, being sure to scrape the bottom of the bowl. Dough may be slightly lumpy.

Drop in 6 large scoops on the baking sheet, at least 3 inches apart. Bake for 10 minutes or until biscuits are puffy and browned. Store leftover biscuits covered at room temperature.

Yield: 6 BISCUITS
Prep time: 20 MINUTES
Difficulty:

BETTAH CHETTAH BISCUITS

These cheesy biscuits are wonderful with a slab of margarine in the middle or crumbled over a bowl of soup.

2 cups flour
¼ cup nutritional yeast
2 teaspoons baking powder
¼ teaspoon salt
⅛ teaspoon powdered garlic
2 tablespoons margarine, melted
2 tablespoon light miso
¾ cup milk

Preheat the oven to 400 degrees. Line a baking sheet with parchment paper.

In a large bowl, combine flour, nutritional yeast, baking powder, salt and powdered garlic. In a small bowl, whisk together melted margarine and miso. Add milk and whisk to break up miso. Add wet ingredients to dry ingredients and mix until just incorporated.

You can either drop the batter onto a baking sheet in ½ cup-sized blobs or roll out dough on a well-floured surface and cut into 6 rounds using a biscuit cutter. Bake for 18 to 22 minutes, until biscuits are lightly browned. Store leftover biscuits covered at room temperature.

Yield: 6 BISCUITS
Prep time: 25 MINUTES
Difficulty:

CAKES

Hooray for cake! Cakes can seem large and labor-intensive, but they don't take up nearly as much time as other desserts do and the end product is oh-so-impressive. I always line the bottoms of my cake pans with parchment paper to ensure that the cakes come out nicely. It also keeps the bottoms of the cakes moist. If you don't have parchment paper, greasing and flouring the pans usually works fine.

- CINN-FUL APPLE CAKE
- PEANUT BUTTER BANANA CAKE
- MARBLED BUNDT CAKE
- FOREVER CARROT CAKE
- PUMPKIN-CINNAMON SWIRL CHEESECAKE
- CHERRY CLAFOUTIS
- CHOCO-CHAI COFFEE CAKE
- PEACH BUNDT COFFEE CAKE
- BEST BOSTON CREAM PIE
- CHOCOLATE ORANGE CREAM LOAF CAKE
- BLACKEST FOREST CAKE
- TROPICAL COCONUT CAKE
- ALMOST-FLOURLESS KAHLÚA CAKE
- RED VELVET CUPCAKES
- BANANA SPLIT CUPCAKES

Cinn-ful Apple Cake

This cake is deliciously simple. No frosting to worry about, no layers to stack, just a straightforward cake filled with chunks of apples and with a crunchy cinnamon-sugar topping. Looks are deceiving with this cake; it seems kind of plain, but it packs a flavorful punch.

1 ½ cups flour

2 teaspoons baking powder

¼ teaspoon salt

1 ¾ cups sugar, divided

½ cup margarine, melted and cooled

¾ cup applesauce

1 teaspoon vanilla

¼ cup milk

2 teaspoons cinnamon

3 cups peeled, chopped baking apples (such as Granny Smith)

Preheat the oven to 350 degrees. Grease and flour the sides of an 8-inch springform pan and line the bottom with parchment paper. If you do not have a springform pan, a regular 8-inch cake pan will do.

In a small bowl, combine flour, baking powder and salt. In a large bowl, cream together 1 ¼ cups sugar with margarine. Add applesauce. Incorporate vanilla and milk until mixed through. Add dry ingredients to wet ingredients in two batches until just mixed.

Combine cinnamon with remaining ¼ cup sugar. Toss 2 tablespoons cinnamon-sugar mixture with sliced apples. Gently fold apples into batter.

Spread batter in the prepared pan. Sprinkle top with remaining cinnamon-sugar mixture. Bake for 65 to 70 minutes, until middle of cake is set and a toothpick comes out clean. Remove cake and let cool completely on a cooling rack before serving. Store cake covered at room temperature.

Yield: 1 CAKE, 12 SLICES
Prep time: 20 MINUTES
Difficulty:

PEANUT BUTTER BANANA CAKE

This cake is fit for a king, and I don't mean Elvis, although I'm sure he would have liked it! The taste and texture of this cake is all about subtlety. Serve it with a drizzle of warm melted chocolate and some fresh banana slices, and it's sure to be a dessert-time hit!

2 cups flour

2 teaspoons baking powder

1 teaspoon baking soda

½ teaspoon salt

⅔ cup melted margarine, cooled to room temperature

1¼ cups brown sugar, packed

1 teaspoon vanilla

4 mashed bananas

½ cup milk

1 teaspoon mild vinegar

1 recipe Peanut Butter Frosting (page 156)

2 bananas, sliced

Preheat the oven to 350 degrees. Lightly grease and flour two 9-inch cake pans and line the bottoms with parchment paper.

In a small bowl, combine flour, baking powder, baking soda and salt. In a large bowl, mix melted margarine and brown sugar. Add vanilla and bananas. In a small bowl, add vinegar to milk and let sit for a couple of minutes. Add dry ingredients to wet ingredients in two batches, then stir in milk mixture. Mix batter until just combined and divide evenly into the baking pans.

Bake for 25 to 30 minutes, until cakes are lightly browned and a toothpick comes out clean. Cool in the pan for 20 minutes, then invert onto a rack to finish cooling.

Frost with Peanut Butter Frosting using a thick layer of frosting and a layer of sliced fresh bananas between the cakes. This cake is extra delicious with warm chocolate sauce drizzled on top. Simply melt chocolate chips and serve! Store leftover cake covered in the fridge.

Yield: 1 DOUBLE-LAYER CAKE, 12 SLICES
Prep time: 30 MINUTES
Difficulty:

MARBLED BUNDT CAKE

This Bundt cake is the perfect blend of vanilla and chocolate. Topped with a little sifting of powdered sugar, this is a simple cake that has a beautiful presentation and pairs perfectly with your favorite coffee or tea.

3 cups flour

1½ cups sugar

1 teaspoon baking powder

1 teaspoon baking soda

¼ teaspoon salt

1½ cups milk, divided

1 teaspoon mild vinegar

1 teaspoon vanilla

¾ cup oil

½ cup baking cocoa

½ cup chocolate chips

Preheat the oven to 350 degrees. Lightly grease and flour a Bundt pan.

In a medium bowl, combine flour, sugar, baking powder, baking soda and salt. In a large bowl, combine 1¼ cups milk and vinegar and let sit for a couple of minutes. Add vanilla and oil and mix to combine. Add dry ingredients to wet ingredients in two batches until just mixed. Divide batter between two bowls.

In a separate small bowl, combine cocoa and remaining ¼ cup milk. Add this mixture and chocolate chips to one of the batter halves and mix until just incorporated. Alternate adding scoops of vanilla batter and chocolate batter to the Bundt pan. Draw a knife through the batter several times to swirl.

Bake for 40 to 45 minutes, until a toothpick comes out clean. Let cake cool in the pan on a cooling rack, then invert onto a plate or platter. Store leftover cake covered at room temperature.

Yield: 1 CAKE, 12 SLICES
Prep time: 20 MINUTES
Difficulty:

FOREVER CARROT CAKE

Jim and I had carrot cake at our wedding, so this recipe is especially significant to us. I think it strikes a nice balance between deep and spicy and light and fluffy. This recipe makes a beautiful double-layer cake. Don't be afraid to put a generous smear of Cream Cheese Frosting between the layers, because there is more than enough to frost the whole cake. The spices really set up overnight, so this cake tastes best the next day. If you can't wait, though, I don't blame you.

$2\frac{1}{4}$ cups all-purpose flour

2 teaspoons baking powder

1 teaspoon baking soda

2 teaspoons pumpkin pie spice

2 teaspoons cinnamon

$\frac{1}{2}$ teaspoon salt

$\frac{1}{2}$ cup oil

$\frac{1}{2}$ cup brown sugar, packed

$\frac{1}{2}$ cup sugar

2 cups finely grated carrots

1 cup applesauce

$\frac{1}{3}$ cup milk

1 teaspoon vanilla

$\frac{1}{3}$ cup walnuts

$\frac{1}{3}$ cup raisins

1 recipe Cream Cheese Frosting (page 155)

Preheat the oven to 350 degrees. Grease and flour the sides and bottoms of two 9-inch cake pans and line the bottoms with parchment paper.

In a small bowl, combine flour, baking powder, baking soda, pumpkin pie spice, cinnamon and salt. In a large bowl, combine oil, sugar and brown sugar. Add carrots, applesauce, milk and vanilla and mix well. Add dry ingredients to wet ingredients in two batches, then stir in nuts and raisins until just mixed. Divide batter between the two pans.

Bake for 25 to 28 minutes, until cakes are golden and a toothpick comes out clean. Cool on cooling racks in the pans for 20 minutes, run a knife around the outside of the cakes, then invert the pans and finish cooling cakes directly on racks. Spread a thick layer of Cream Cheese Frosting between cooled cakes and frost the top and sides. Store leftover cake covered in the fridge.

Yield: 1 DOUBLE-LAYER CAKE, 8 TO 10 SLICES
Prep time: 30 MINUTES
Difficulty:

Pumpkin-Cinnamon Swirl Cheesecake

I love pumpkin. The only thing I love more than pumpkin is cheesecake. The combination is a Thanksgiving masterpiece. You'll want to save room for this one: a moist, dense cheesecake mixed with spiced pumpkin swirls and laced with intense cinnamon ribbons.

CRUST:

¾ cup flour

1 teaspoon pumpkin pie spice

¼ cup brown sugar

⅓ cup margarine, softened

1 teaspoon molasses

1 tablespoon milk

FILLING:

2 8-ounce containers
soy cream cheese

1 aseptic container firm tofu

1 cup sugar, divided

3 tablespoons cornstarch, divided

2 teaspoons vanilla

1 cup pumpkin purée
(not pumpkin pie mix)

2 teaspoons pumpkin pie spice

1 teaspoon milk

1 tablespoon cinnamon

- -

For plain cheesecake, make the crust without pumpkin pie spice and mix the filling without pumpkin purée, pumpkin pie spice or cinnamon and add ⅓ cup additional sugar and 1 teaspoon lemon juice. Serve with the cherry topping from Blackest Forest Cake (page 94) or the strawberry topping from Strawberry Lemonade Cheesepie (page 104).

Preheat the oven to 350 degrees. Lightly grease the bottom and sides of a 9-inch springform pan.

For Crust: In a small bowl, mix together flour, pumpkin pie spice and brown sugar. Add margarine, molasses and milk and stir until crumbly. Press mixture into the bottom of the prepared pan and bake for 12 minutes.

For Filling: While crust is baking, combine cream cheese, tofu, ½ cup sugar, 2 tablespoons cornstarch and vanilla in a food processor or blender. Blend until well-incorporated, scraping down the sides of the bowl as needed. Pour 1½ cups of mixture into a bowl and set aside. Add remaining ½ cup sugar, remaining 1 tablespoon cornstarch, pumpkin purée and pumpkin pie spice. Process until well-blended.

From reserved filling, reserve 3 tablespoons in a small bowl. Add milk and cinnamon to the reserved 3 tablespoons. Mix well to incorporate.

For Assembly: In the springform pan, alternate adding ½ cup vanilla filling and ½ cup pumpkin filling on top of the crust. Drizzle cinnamon mixture on top of filling in thick stripes. Lightly wiggle the pan to help the contents settle. Draw a knife though the batter several times to marble.

Bake for 45 to 50 minutes, until center of filling is set but still slightly jiggly. Let cake cool completely then let set in the fridge for at least 2 hours before serving. Best if made the night before so the spices have time to meld. Store leftover cake covered in the fridge.

Yield: 12 SLICES

Prep time: 35 MINUTES

Difficulty: 🥄🥄🥄🥄

CHERRY CLAFOUTIS

The Cherry Clafoutis is considered to be the national cake of France, although it's actually more like a custard baked in a pie dish. If anyone knows pastries and baked goods, though, it's the French, so I'm not about to question it! This cherry-filled treat is very light and creamy and can be passed off as a foreign breakfast if anyone asks why you're eating leftover slices at 6 a.m.

½ aseptic package firm silken tofu

⅓ cup sugar

½ cup flour

1 teaspoon baking powder

¼ teaspoon salt

1 cup milk, divided

1 teaspoon vanilla

1½ cups cherries (pitted, if fresh; thawed and drained, if frozen; or drained and rinsed, if canned)

Preheat the oven to 425 degrees. Lightly grease a 9-inch pie dish with margarine or oil.

In a food processor, purée tofu and sugar until smooth. Add flour, baking powder, salt and ½ cup milk. Purée until smooth. Add remaining ½ cup milk and vanilla and process until smooth.

Pour batter into prepared pie dish and sprinkle cherries evenly across top of batter. Bake for 15 minutes at 425 degrees, then lower the oven temperature to 350 degrees and bake for an additional 20 to 25 minutes, until edges of clafoutis are set and middle is still a little jiggly. Let cool on a cooling rack for at least 25 minutes before serving. Best served warm. Store leftover clafoutis covered in the fridge.

Yield: 1 CAKE, 12 SLICES
Prep time: 25 MINUTES
Difficulty: 🥄 🥄

CHOCO-CHAI COFFEE CAKE

This flavor-infused rendition of classic coffee cake has hints of the East in its complex spices and has the tradition of the West in its form. It makes a great breakfast or dessert (or dessert for breakfast).

BATTER:

4 to 5 chai tea bags

1 ¾ cups warm milk

3 ½ cups flour

1 ½ cups sugar

1 tablespoon baking powder

1 teaspoon baking soda

1 teaspoon salt

1 teaspoon cinnamon

⅓ cup oil

½ cup plus 2 tablespoons yogurt
(equal to 1 6-ounce container)

1 teaspoon vanilla

TOPPING:

½ cup flour

6 tablespoons brown sugar

3 tablespoons baking cocoa

4 tablespoons cold margarine

1 cup chocolate chips

Preheat the oven to 350 degrees. Lightly grease an 11 × 13-inch baking pan with margarine or oil, or line it with parchment paper.

For Batter: In a small bowl, steep tea bags in warm milk for at least 5 minutes. Squeeze out bags and let milk cool. In a large bowl, combine flour, sugar, baking powder, baking soda, salt and cinnamon. In a medium bowl, combine oil with sugar until creamy. Add yogurt, vanilla and cooled chai milk. Add wet ingredients to dry ingredients and combine until just mixed.

For Topping: In a small bowl, combine cocoa with brown sugar and flour. Cut in margarine with your fingers or a pastry cutter until mixture is crumbly. Add chocolate chips.

For Assembly: Spread batter in the baking pan. Sprinkle on topping and bake for 35 to 40 minutes, until cake is set on the edges and toothpick comes out clean. Store leftover cake covered at room temperature.

Yield: 20 SLICES
Prep time: 25 MINUTES
Difficulty:

PEACH BUNDT COFFEE CAKE

This Bundt cake is so delicious: The peach chunks burst with juicy flavor and the cinnamon filling makes for an unexpected treat in the center.

FOR BATTER:

3 cups flour

2 teaspoons baking powder

½ teaspoon salt

1⅔ cups sugar

¾ cup oil

½ cup plus 2 tablespoons yogurt (equal to 1 6-ounce container)

1 teaspoon vanilla

½ cup milk

½ teaspoon mild vinegar

1½ cups chopped peaches (fresh, frozen, or canned and well-drained)

FILLING:

⅔ cup sugar

1 tablespoon cinnamon

⅓ cup pecans, chopped

Preheat the oven to 350 degrees. Lightly grease and flour a Bundt pan.

For Batter: In a medium bowl, combine flour, baking powder and salt. In a large bowl, combine sugar and oil. Add yogurt and vanilla and mix until well-incorporated. Add milk and vinegar and let sit for 2 minutes. Add dry ingredients to wet ingredients in two batches. Fold in peaches and combine until just incorporated.

For Filling: In a small bowl, combine sugar, cinnamon and pecans.

For Assembly: Spread half of batter in the Bundt pan. Sprinkle filling around the middle of the first layer, then spread the remaining batter on top.

Bake for about 50 to 55 minutes or until a toothpick comes out clean. Let cool in the pan for about 25 minutes, then invert onto a cooling rack to finish cooling. Dust with powdered sugar or lightly glaze with White Icing (page 155) if desired. Store leftover cake covered at room temperature.

Yield: 1 CAKE, 12 SLICES
Prep time: 25 MINUTES
Difficulty:

BEST BOSTON CREAM PIE

With its moist cake layers, creamy custard filling and rich ganache, Boston Cream Pie is a classic treat. I know that you will be antsy to eat this cake, but it's very important that you wait for the filling and ganache to cool completely before assembling the final product.

BATTER:

2 cups flour, sifted

1 teaspoon baking powder

1 teaspoon baking soda

½ teaspoon salt

1¼ cups sugar

½ cup oil

½ cup plus 2 tablespoons yogurt (equal to 1 6-ounce container)

2 teaspoons vanilla

1½ cups milk

FILLING:

⅓ cup sugar

⅛ teaspoon salt

2 tablespoons plus 1 teaspoon cornstarch

1½ cups milk

1 teaspoon margarine

1 teaspoon vanilla

1 recipe Chocolate Ganache (page 159)

. . . .

Most Boston Cream Pies at the grocery store come with a little plastic strip running around the cakes to hold them upright very nicely. You can make your own version of this using a long piece of waxed paper, trimmed to the height of the cake, and a piece of tape.

. . . .

Add two sliced bananas to the cream filling in the middle layer and frost the whole thing with Buttercream Frosting (page 157) to make Banana Cream Cake!

Preheat the oven to 350 degrees. Grease and flour two 9-inch cake pans and line the bottoms with parchment paper.

For Batter: In a medium bowl, combine flour, baking powder, baking soda and salt. In a large bowl, combine sugar and oil. Add yogurt and vanilla and mix until creamy. Stir in milk. Add dry ingredients to wet ingredients in two batches and mix until combined.

Evenly divide batter between the two pans and bake for 20 to 25 minutes, until cakes are golden and a toothpick comes out clean. Let cool on a cooling rack.

For Filling: While the cake layers are cooling, prepare cream filling. In a saucepan, combine sugar, salt and cornstarch. Add milk and whisk together. Bring mixture to a gentle boil over medium heat, whisking constantly. Lower to a simmer and whisk until thickened, about 7 minutes. Remove from heat and add margarine and vanilla. Pour into a bowl and let cool completely, stirring every few minutes. Filling will continue to thicken as it cools.

For Assembly: Spread cream filling between cake layers. Top cake with Chocolate Ganache. Let cake set in the fridge for at least 45 minutes, and remove from the fridge 20 minutes before serving to let ganache soften for easier cutting. Store leftover cake covered in the fridge.

Yield: 1 CAKE, 10 SLICES

Prep time: 45 MINUTES

Difficulty:

CHOCOLATE ORANGE CREAM LOAF CAKE

I know, the words "Loaf Cake" don't suggest much elegance, but this dense triple-layer cake is sure to impress in both looks and taste. The rectangular size is a nice change of pace, and with the creamy orange filling and ganache, it tastes like a million bucks. This cake was born to be eaten with a steaming cup of coffee.

BATTER:

1½ cups flour

⅓ cup baking cocoa, sifted

1 cup sugar

1 teaspoon baking soda

½ teaspoon baking powder

¼ teaspoon salt

⅓ cup oil

¼ cup chocolate chips, melted

1 cup milk

1 teaspoon mild-tasting vinegar

1 teaspoon vanilla

FILLING:

⅓ cup plus 1 tablespoon sugar

2 tablespoons cornstarch

⅔ cup milk

juice of 2 oranges (about ⅓ cup)

½ teaspoon vanilla

1 to 2 teaspoons orange zest, to taste

½ recipe Chocolate Ganache (page 159)

Preheat the oven to 350 degrees. Lightly grease a 9 × 5-inch loaf pan.

For Batter: In a medium bowl, combine flour, cocoa, sugar, baking soda, baking powder and salt. In a large bowl, combine oil, melted chocolate chips, milk, vinegar and vanilla. Mix until combined; it's okay if the oil separates a little. Mix dry ingredients into wet ingredients in two batches until just combined.

Spread batter in loaf pan. Bake for 45 minutes or until a toothpick comes out clean. Let cool on a cooling rack for 20 minutes before running a knife along the edges to loosen and inverting cake directly onto the rack. Let cake cool completely.

For Filling: While cake is cooling, prepare orange-cream filling. In a saucepan, whisk together sugar and cornstarch. Whisk in milk and heat over medium-high heat, whisking constantly, until boiling, about 7 minutes. Add orange juice. Lower heat to medium-low and continue whisking until mixture thickens, about 5 minutes. Add orange zest and vanilla and cook for 1 more minute. Remove from heat and pour into a bowl. Let orange cream cool completely in the fridge, stirring every few minutes to keep a skin from forming on top. If filling begins to clump, whisk rapidly for a few seconds to make it creamy again.

Prepare Chocolate Ganache.

For Assembly: All elements should be completely cool. Level cake by evenly cutting off the top. Cut cake into three even layers. This is easiest to do using unflavored dental floss (fun baking trick!) or a very thin knife. Place bottom layer of cake onto the serving platter you will be using. Spread half of orange-cream filling on top. Add the middle layer of cake. Spread on the rest of the orange cream. Put on top cake layer and frost with cooled ganache. To serve, cut into thin slices and turn onto plate. Store leftover cake covered in the fridge.

Yield: 1 CAKE, 8 TO 10 SLICES
Prep time: 1 HOUR
Difficulty: 🥄🥄🥄🥄

BLACKEST FOREST CAKE

This cake not only tastes great but looks very impressive as well. The recipe is a little unconventional, but it makes a very moist chocolate cake. It is based on a recipe my great-grandmother used to make. Feel free to play with the fruit topping if cherries aren't your thing.

BATTER:

1¾ cups all-purpose flour, sifted

1½ cups sugar

¾ cup baking cocoa

1½ teaspoons baking soda

1½ teaspoons baking powder

⅛ teaspoon salt

½ cup plus 2 tablespoons yogurt (equal to 1 6-ounce container)

1 cup milk

½ cup oil

2 teaspoons vanilla

1 cup boiling water

TOPPING:

⅓ cup sugar

3 tablespoons cornstarch

1 bag frozen cherries (about 2½ cups)

⅓ cup water

1 recipe Chocolate Frosting (page 156)

· ·

Add 1½ cups raspberries to the batter and bake in an 11 x 13-inch pan for an additional 10 minutes, then top with Buttercream Frosting (page 157) to make Chocolate Raspberry Cake!

· ·

Spread a thin layer of peanut butter and a half-recipe of Chocolate Ganache (page 159) between the layers. Frost with Peanut Butter Frosting (page 156) to make Inverted Peanut Butter Cup Cake!

Preheat the oven to 350 degrees. Lightly grease and flour two 9-inch cake pans then line bottoms with parchment paper.

For Batter: In a large bowl, combine flour, sugar, cocoa, baking soda, baking powder and salt. In a separate bowl, mix yogurt, milk, oil and vanilla. Add wet ingredients to dry ones, beating with an electric hand mixer on low speed. Add boiling water and mix to combine. Batter will look very thin.

Ladle batter evenly into cake pans. Bake for 30 to 35 minutes or until a toothpick comes out clean. Cool cake in the pans on a cooling rack before inverting and turning out directly onto the rack to cool completely.

For Topping: In a saucepan, combine sugar with cornstarch until cornstarch is no longer clumpy. Add cherries and water and cook on medium heat, stirring continuously, until mixture is boiling. Let boil, stirring continuously, for about 5 to 7 minutes or until mixture is thickened and coats the back of a spoon without running off. Remove from heat and pour into a heat-safe bowl to cool completely.

For Assembly: Place bottom cake layer on serving platter and spread a thick layer of Chocolate Frosting on top. Carefully center the second layer over the first and spread another thick layer of frosting on the top and down the sides. Spread or pipe frosting around the edge. Cover the center of the top of the cake with cherries. Garnish with chocolate shavings or a dusting of cocoa powder. Store leftover cake covered in the fridge.

Yield: 12 SLICES

Prep time: 30 MINUTES

Difficulty: 🥄🥄🥄

TROPICAL COCONUT CAKE

This is a really refreshing treat, perfect for a summery potluck or for a pick-me-up on a cold winter's day. Use a springform pan for this cake, if you have one. If not, just line the bottom of a cake pan with parchment paper, otherwise the mandarin oranges will stick.

1½ cups flour

2 teaspoons baking soda

⅛ teaspoon salt

1 cup sugar

⅓ cup oil

1 cup milk

1 tablespoon vanilla

1 teaspoon mild vinegar

2 small cans mandarin oranges, well-drained and chopped

1 recipe Coconut Glaze (page 158)

. . . .

Never fear if the oranges sink a little in this cake. Each bite is incredibly moist and the glaze looks beautiful.

Preheat the oven to 350 degrees. Lightly grease and flour a 9-inch springform pan or a 9-inch cake pan and line it with parchment paper.

In a large bowl, combine flour, baking soda and salt. In a small bowl, combine sugar and oil. Add milk, vanilla and vinegar. Combine wet ingredients with dry ingredients and fold in mandarin oranges until just mixed.

Spread batter into prepared pan. Bake for 30 to 35 minutes or until cake looks browned and springs back when you touch it and the toothpick comes out clean. Cool completely on rack and top with Coconut Glaze and shredded coconut. Store leftover cake covered at room temperature.

Yield: 1 CAKE, 10 TO 12 SLICES
Prep time: 20 MINUTES
Difficulty:

ALMOST-FLOURLESS KAHLÚA CAKE

This cake has just a little bit of flour, but it is incredibly creamy and chocolatey, with a richness similar to a cheesecake. It's incredibly easy to throw together and is versatile. You can experiment with other liqueurs besides Kahlúa to mix things up. If you are leery about baking with tofu, I can understand your hesitation; it used to scare me, too. I can assure you that you could feed this cake to anyone and they'd never know what's in it. This cake is baked in a water bath to keep it from cracking on top.

3 aseptic packages firm tofu
1¼ cups sugar
1 tablespoon lemon juice
½ cup chocolate chips, melted
¼ cup baking cocoa
⅓ cup Kahlúa
3 tablespoons flour
½ teaspoon vanilla

Preheat the oven to 350 degrees. Lightly grease the sides and bottom of a 9-inch springform pan and wrap foil around the bottom outside edge to cover the seal between the bottom and the sides. Bring a large pot of water to a simmer for the water bath.

In a food processor or blender, process tofu, sugar, lemon juice, melted chocolate chips, cocoa, Kahlúa, flour and vanilla until smooth, scraping down the sides of the bowl as needed. Pour mixture into the springform pan. Place the springform pan inside of another larger pan with high sides. Pour enough hot water into the outer pan to reach the middle of the springform pan. Your springform pan should look like it is surrounded by water.

Bake for 1 hour. If water evaporates while it is baking, be sure to refill the pan with hot water only, especially if you are using a glass dish; the temperature shock could cause the glass to break. Cool cake completely in the pan on a cooling rack and then let set in fridge for 2 hours before serving. This cake is best if left to sit overnight. Store leftover cake covered in the fridge.

Yield: 12 SLICES
Prep time: 15 MINUTES
Difficulty:

Red Velvet Cupcakes

These cupcakes look quite elegant with their deep, red color poking out of the liners and their creamy white frosting on top. Red Velvet Cake has a signature richness and dense crumb, and these cuppers don't disappoint.

1½ cups flour, sifted

2 tablespoons baking cocoa, sifted

1 teaspoon baking soda

¼ teaspoon baking powder

¼ teaspoon salt

½ cup margarine, softened

¾ cup sugar

½ cup plus 2 tablespoons yogurt (equal to 1 6-ounce container)

1 cup milk

1 teaspoon mild vinegar

½ teaspoon vanilla

2 to 3 tablespoons red food coloring, depending on how red you want the cupcakes to be

1 recipe Buttercream Frosting (page 157)

. . . .

Use blue food coloring instead of red and top your treats with Peanut Butter Frosting (page 156) for Velvet Elvis Cupcakes that would make The King proud.

Preheat the oven to 350 degrees. Line 12 muffin cups with paper liners.

In a medium bowl, sift together flour, cocoa, baking soda, baking powder and salt. In a large bowl, cream together margarine and sugar with an electric hand mixer. Add yogurt, milk and vinegar and mix until combined. Add vanilla and food coloring and mix, scraping down the sides of the bowl until well-combined. Add dry ingredients to wet ingredients in two batches and mix until well-combined, about 1 minute.

Fill muffin cups ⅔ of the way full with batter. Bake for 15 to 18 minutes or until a toothpick comes out clean. Let cool completely on a cooling rack before frosting with Butter Cream Frosting. Store cupcakes covered at room temperature.

Yield: 12 CUPCAKES
Prep Time: 20 MINUTES
Difficulty:

BANANA SPLIT CUPCAKES

These cupcakes are completely addictive and this is the one recipe I kept "testing" long after it was perfected. For anyone who loves banana splits, these are the absolute best, whether you're a kid or just a kid at heart. They are delicious plain, because they're so moist and flavorful, or you can frost them. This recipe also makes a great 9 x 9-inch sheet cake.

1 ½ cups flour

2 teaspoons baking powder

¼ teaspoon salt

⅓ cup oil

½ cup plus 2 tablespoons yogurt (equal to 1 6-ounce container)

¾ cup sugar

1 teaspoon vanilla

1 8-ounce can crushed pineapple, drained

½ cup chocolate chips

¼ cup maraschino cherries, drained and chopped

1 ½ bananas, in ¼-inch slices

¼ cup salted peanuts

Preheat the oven to 350 degrees. Line 12 muffin cups with paper liners.

In a large bowl, combine flour, baking powder and salt. In a medium bowl, mix together oil, yogurt, sugar and vanilla until well-combined. Add wet ingredients to dry ingredients and mix until just incorporated. Gently fold in pineapple, chocolate chips and cherries. Add banana slices and mix carefully.

Spoon batter into muffin tin almost to the top of each cup. Bake for 22 to 24 minutes (35 to 40 minutes for a 9 x 9-inch sheet cake), until cupcakes are lightly browned and a toothpick comes out clean. Let cupcakes cool on a cooling rack.

Cupcakes can be served plain, warm with a scoop of ice cream and a sprinkling of peanuts, or frosted with Butter Cream Frosting with peanuts sprinkled on top. Store leftover cupcakes covered at room temperature.

Yield: 12 CUPCAKES
Prep time: 20 MINUTES
Difficulty:

PIES & TARTS

P ie in the sky, my oh my! For the longest time, I thought I didn't like pie. I had tried many kinds, but nothing really clicked. Crafting pies in my own kitchen, I learned that they are an art form unto themselves and that a well-made pie is, well, blissful. Don't be afraid to try making your own crust; it's very simple, especially if you have a food processor. Pies exude a certain unparalleled homemade comfort. For your next holiday or special occasion, try treating your loved ones to a pie.

- BASIC PIE CRUST
- CRAN-APPLE PIE
- GAS STATION PIE
- PUMP-CAN PIE
- STRAWBERRY LEMONADE CHEESEPIE
- RASPBERRY PEACH LATTICE PIE
- MIXED BERRY PIE
- PEAR CHOCOLATE CREAM GALETTE
- POLSKI APPLE CRISP
- CHOCOLATE STRAWBERRY TART
- LEMON ALMOND TORTE
- CHOCOLATE WALNUT TOFFEE TORTE

BASIC PIE CRUST

This classic basic pie crust is very versatile for all your pie-making needs. It holds together well enough to make lattice tops (like for Raspberry Peach Lattice Pie, page 106) but bakes up buttery and light.

2½ cups flour
½ teaspoon salt
1 teaspoon sugar
1 cup cold margarine, chopped into chunks
¼ to ½ cup cold water

. . . .

Use half margarine and half shortening for a flakier, but slightly more delicate, crust.

. . . .

This recipe makes enough dough for two single-crust pies (like Cran-Apple Pie or Pump-Can Pie) or for one double-crust pie (like Mixed Berry Pie). Remember that if you only need half a recipe's worth, you can freeze the other half of the dough for up to 2 weeks.

If using a food processor, pulse together flour, salt, sugar and margarine until margarine is blended and mixture resembles a coarse meal. With food processor running, add just enough cold water to form a soft dough. Dough should hold together but not be sticky.

If making by hand, in a large bowl, combine flour, salt and sugar. With a fork or pastry cutter, cut in margarine until mixture resembles a coarse meal, with pieces no bigger than the size of a pea. Add just enough cold water and mix until a smooth dough pulls together. Dough should hold together but not be sticky.

Divide dough into two discs and wrap in plastic wrap. Chill in the fridge for at least 1 hour before using, or freeze for up to 2 weeks. Keep dough in the fridge until you're ready to use it.

Yield: 2 CRUSTS
Prep time: 5 MINUTES ACTIVE, AT LEAST 1 HOUR INACTIVE
Difficulty: ✎ WITH A FOOD PROCESSOR,
✎✎ WITHOUT A FOOD PROCESSOR

CRAN-APPLE PIE

This pie is ridiculously simple to make and yields delectable results. So toss it in the oven and prepare to be showered with praise by your dinner guests.

½ recipe Basic Pie Crust (1 pie crust)

FILLING:

4 large baking apples, peeled

½ cup sugar

⅓ cup fresh or frozen cranberries

2 teaspoons lemon juice

1½ teaspoons cinnamon

TOPPING:

⅓ cup flour

⅓ cup brown sugar

3 tablespoons cold margarine

Preheat the oven to 375 degrees. Roll out pie crust to 12 inches in diameter and fit to a 9-inch pie dish.

For Filling: Core apples and slice into ½-inch wedges. In a large bowl, toss together apple slices, sugar, cranberries and lemon juice. Sprinkle with cinnamon and toss to combine. Spread filling into prepared pie crust so apples are in an even layer.

For Topping: In a small bowl, combine flour, brown sugar and margarine with the back of a fork, until mixture is crumbly. Sprinkle on top of pie filling.

Bake for 1 hour to 1 hour and 10 minutes, until topping is browned and filling is bubbly. You may need to put a baking sheet lined with foil on the oven rack under the pie to catch any drips from the filling. Let pie cool completely before serving so filling can set. Store leftover pie covered at room temperature.

Yield: 1 PIE, 8 SLICES

Prep time: 35 MINUTES

Difficulty:

GAS STATION PIE

When I was a kid, I loved those hand-held Hostess pies that you can get at gas stations. They were one of my favorite things to eat, and when presented with the opportunity to have one, I was always stumped over which filling to get. I would linger and debate over which one to choose in the way kids do, when they go on and on in hopes of an adult saying, "Oh, just get both!" These little portable pies are a serious step up from those gas-station versions, and you're sure to love them as much as I do. Feel free to play around with the filling and try other things, like the filling from Strawberry Lemonade Cheesepie (page 104).

½ recipe Basic Pie Crust (1 crust)

¼ cup sugar

2 teaspoons cornstarch

¼ teaspoon cinnamon

2 cups peeled, chopped apples
(approximately 1 large apple)

2 tablespoons water

1 tablespoon milk

¾ to 1 cup powdered sugar

. . . .

Fill your pies with the filling from Best Boston Cream Pie (page 91) and glaze them with half a recipe of Chocolate Ganache (page 159) to make Bavarian Cream Pies!

Preheat the oven to 375 degrees. Line a baking sheet with parchment paper. Keep dough chilled in fridge until ready to use.

In a saucepan, combine sugar, cornstarch and cinnamon. Add apples and water and mix well. Cook over medium heat, stirring often, until apples begin to soften and a thick syrup forms, about 10 minutes. Set aside to cool slightly.

On a lightly floured surface, divide chilled pie crust into three equal balls. Roll each ball out to 6 inches in diameter. Divide the apple filling equally among the crusts, spooning it onto half of each crust and leaving a ½-inch edge for sealing. On the other half of each crust, make a small air vent, about the size of the hole of a straw, with the tip of a knife. Fold the side of the dough with the air vent over the filling and pinch the edges together to make a firm seal. You may need to use a little water to moisten the dough and get a good seal. Each pie should now look like a half-circle.

Place pies on the baking sheet and bake for 22 to 25 minutes, until lightly golden. Transfer to a cooling rack.

While pies are cooling, whisk together milk and powdered sugar to make a thick but brushable icing. Brush icing onto the top of each warm pie and let pies cool completely. Store leftover pies covered at room temperature.

Yield: 3 SMALL PIES
Prep time: 40 MINUTES
Difficulty: 🥄🥄🥄

PUMP-CAN PIE

While I love pumpkin, I've never been a huge pumpkin pie fan. I do love pecan pie, though. Because they are both such Thanksgiving staples, I thought why not combine the two into a pie powerhouse? This combination is fantastic, and by uniting the pumpkin and pecan pie, you save more room for seconds!

½ recipe **Basic Pie Crust** (1 crust)

1 15-ounce can plus 1 cup pumpkin purée (not pumpkin pie mix)

¼ cup milk

1¼ brown sugar

2 tablespoons cornstarch

3 tablespoons molasses

2 teaspoons pumpkin pie spice

2 teaspoons cinnamon

1 teaspoon vanilla

½ teaspoon maple extract (optional)

½ teaspoon salt

1 cup pecan halves

Preheat the oven to 400 degrees.

Roll out chilled pie crust to 12 inches in diameter. Set pie crust in a 9-inch pie dish and trim and crimp edges. Poke crust with the tines of a fork in several places. Put a sheet of parchment paper on top of crust and fill with pie weights or 2 cups dried beans. Bake for 12 to 15 minutes, until crust looks a little dry. Let crust cool on a cooling rack and remove the beans or pie weights.

After crust has cooled for about 20 minutes, prepare the pie filling. In a food processor or blender, purée pumpkin, milk and brown sugar until well-combined. Add cornstarch, molasses, pumpkin pie spice, cinnamon, vanilla, salt and maple extract, if using. Process until smooth and all ingredients are incorporated, scraping down sides of food processor as needed. Pour filling into pie crust and arrange pecans on top.

Cover pie with foil and bake for 25 minutes. Remove foil and continue baking for an additional 25 to 30 minutes, until edges are set and center is still a little jiggly. Let cool completely before serving. Best if made the night before to let spices set. Store leftover pie covered at room temperature.

Yield: 1 PIE, 8 SLICES
Prep time: 40 MINUTES
Difficulty: ✎✎

STRAWBERRY LEMONADE CHEESEPIE

I learned from the all-knowing Internet that when you make a cheesecake in a pie dish you have to call it a "cheesepie" not a "cheesecake." Well, la-ti-da! Lucky for us, this pie is to die for, whichever way you slice it! The pie is baked in a water bath, but don't let that scare you. It's just a simple extra step that guarantees a creamy filling with no cracks.

½ recipe Basic Pie Crust (1 crust)

FILLING:

1 8-ounce container
vegan cream cheese

½ cup plus 2 tablespoons yogurt
(1 6-ounce container)

1 aseptic container firm silken tofu

1 cup sugar

1 teaspoon vanilla

1 teaspoon lemon zest

2 tablespoons lemon juice

. . . .

Instead of lemon, add the zest of 2 oranges and the juice of 1 orange. Top with half a recipe of Chocolate Ganache (page 159) to make Chocolate Orange Cheesepie.

Preheat the oven to 350 degrees.

Roll out chilled pie crust to about 12 inches in diameter and place in a 9-inch pie dish. Trim and crimp edges and poke crust with the tines of a fork in several places. Put a sheet of parchment paper on top of crust and fill with pie weights or 2 cups dried beans and bake for 10 minutes. Let crust cool on a cooling rack and remove the beans or pie weights.

For Filling: Purée cream cheese, yogurt, tofu and sugar in a food processor or blender until smooth, scraping down sides as needed. Add vanilla, lemon zest and lemon juice until incorporated. Pour mixture into cooled pie crust.

Place pie dish in a large baking pan with high sides. Add enough warm water to the pan to come up to the middle of the side of the pie dish. This is called a water bath, and it will prevent your pie from cracking and will keep it creamy without it getting a skin on top. If the water evaporates while baking, add more as needed, but only add hot water so you do not shock your bakeware and risk it cracking.

Bake pie for 1 hour. Center may not look completely set, but will firm up while cooling. Remove pie from oven and remove from water bath to cool on cooling rack.

TOPPING:

¼ cup sugar

1 tablespoon cornstarch

1¼ cups strawberries, fresh or frozen, chopped

¼ cup water

For Topping: While pie is baking, combine sugar and cornstarch in a sauce pan. Add strawberries and water and stir to combine. Over medium-high heat, bring mixture to a boil, continuously stirring. Once mixture boils, lower heat to medium. Continue stirring, and cook until strawberries become soft and mixture thickens, about 5 to 10 minutes. Remove from heat. Let topping cool completely, occasionally stirring to keep a skin from forming.

Spread cooled strawberry topping on cooled cheesepie. Let set in the fridge for at least 2 hours before serving. Store leftover pie covered in the fridge.

Yield: 1 PIE, 12 SLICES
Prep time: 50 MINUTES
Difficulty:

RASPBERRY PEACH LATTICE PIE

This pie is bursting with summer. Sweet, juicy peaches and tart raspberries under a lattice top will leave you drooling with anticipation while you wait for this pie to cool. You can use fresh or frozen fruit for this recipe.

1 full recipe Basic Pie Crust (2 crusts)

5 cups sliced peaches (peeled, if fresh; slightly thawed, if frozen)

1½ cups raspberries, fresh or frozen

¼ cup cornstarch

¾ cup sugar

Preheat the oven to 375 degrees.

On a lightly floured surface, roll out each pie crust to 12 inches in diameter. Place one pie crust in the bottom of a 9-inch pie dish, letting the edges overhang. Using a pizza cutter or sharp knife, slice the second crust into ¾-inch strips.

In a large bowl, combine peaches and raspberries. In a small bowl, mix together cornstarch and sugar. Sprinkle sugar mixture over fruit and toss to coat. Pour fruit into crust in the pie dish, sprinkling with any remaining sugar mixture. Lay every other strip of the sliced crust across the top of the pie, going up and down. Weave remaining strips of crust through the strips on the pie in the opposite direction, side to side. Once all strips are woven in, trim crust as needed and pinch edges of top to edges of bottom crust to seal. Brush top of lattice with water and sprinkle with sugar.

Cover pie with foil and bake for 30 minutes, if using fresh fruit. Remove foil and bake for 20 to 25 more minutes, until crust is golden and filling is bubbling slightly. If using frozen fruit, bake with the foil cover for 35 minutes. Remove foil and then bake for 25 to 30 more minutes, until crust is golden and filling is bubbling slightly. Remove pie from oven and let cool on a rack completely before serving. Store leftover pie covered at room temperature.

Yield: 1 PIE, 8 TO 10 SLICES
Prep time: 40 MINUTES
Difficulty: 🥄🥄🥄

Mixed Berry Pie

This pie is an absolute classic. A sweet and tart berry filling sandwiched between two flaky crusts is sure to leave you with a blue-lipped smile on your face. Fresh or frozen berries work just fine in this, making it a perfect dessert for any time of year. I typically use blueberries, raspberries and blackberries, but I've been known to throw in some chopped strawberries from time to time.

1 full recipe Basic Pie Crust (2 crusts)

¾ cup sugar

3 tablespoons cornstarch

4 to 4½ cups of berries (gently rinsed, if fresh; slightly thawed, if frozen)

1 teaspoon lemon juice

Preheat the oven to 375 degrees.

On a lightly floured surface, roll out the bottom pie crust to 12 inches in diameter and the top one to 10 inches. Fit the bottom crust in the bottom of a 9-inch pie dish, with edges hanging over the sides. Cut a little air vent in the second crust.

In a large bowl, combine sugar and cornstarch until well-mixed and there are no lumps. Add berries and carefully mix to be sure that all berries are coated with the sugar and cornstarch. Sprinkle on lemon juice. Scoop coated berries into the pie crust, including any remaining sugar mixture. Place the second crust on top of the filling and crimp top crust edges to bottom crust edges and trim excess dough as needed. Brush top crust with milk and sprinkle with a little sugar.

Cover edges of pie with a pie shield or foil. Bake for 30 minutes, then remove the pie shield and let pie bake for 20 to 25 minutes more, until crust is golden. It may require a few more minutes of baking if your berries were frozen. Let pie cool completely before serving to be sure berry filling is set. Store leftover pie covered at room temperature.

Yield: 1 PIE, 8 TO 10 SLICES
Prep time: 20 MINUTES
Difficulty:

PEAR CHOCOLATE CREAM GALETTE

This rustic tart is one of my favorite recipes in the book. Top 10! Okay, maybe Top 20, because I just can't choose. Vanilla, chocolate and pears meld together to perfection in a buttery crust. Once the elements of this tart are ready, you can literally throw them all together and bake up a very classy and amazing treat that is sure to become a classic in your home.

½ recipe Basic Pie Crust (1 crust)

¼ cup plus 1 tablespoon sugar, divided

1½ teaspoons cornstarch

¼ teaspoon salt

½ cup plus 1 teaspoon milk

2 teaspoons vanilla, divided

1 teaspoon lemon juice

3 to 4 peeled firm pears, in ¼-inch slices (about 3 cups)

½ cup chocolate chips, melted

1 teaspoon milk

1 teaspoon sugar

. . . .

Instead of pears and chocolate cream, fill the crust with the filling from Cran-Apple Pie (page 101) to make Cran-Apple Galette!

Preheat the oven to 375 degrees. Line a baking sheet with parchment paper. Keep pie crust cool in the fridge until ready to use.

In a small sauce pan, combine ¼ cup plus 1 tablespoon sugar, cornstarch and salt. Whisk in milk and cook over medium-high heat, whisking constantly, until mixture begins to bubble, approximately 7 to 9 minutes. Lower heat and continue to stir. Let simmer for 4 to 6 minutes, until mixture thickens and coats the back of a spoon without just dripping off. Remove from heat and whisk in vanilla.

In a medium bowl, sprinkle lemon juice over pears. Add sugar and gently mix to coat.

On a lightly floured surface, roll out chilled pie crust to about 10 to 11 inches in diameter. Transfer dough to baking sheet. Spread melted chocolate in center of dough, leaving a 2-inch border around the edge of the crust. Pour vanilla mixture over chocolate. Layer pears on top of filling and fold remaining edge of dough over the top pears to cover, crimping the overlapping edges of dough as needed. Brush the edge with 1 teaspoon milk and sprinkle remaining sugar on top.

Bake for 40 to 45 minutes, until crust is golden. Remove from the oven and let cool at least 25 minutes before serving. Best if cooled completely. Store leftover galette covered in the fridge.

Yield: 1 GALETTE, ABOUT 10 SLICES
Prep time: 40 MINUTES
Difficulty:

POLSKI APPLE CRISP

What's Polish about pecans and apples you ask? Nothing, but this is a variation on an apple crisp recipe I got from my great-great aunt Pauline, just one of the lovely ladies in my Polish family with whom I spent many childhood weekends.

½ cup flour

½ cup oats

½ cup sugar, divided

1 teaspoon cinnamon

¼ teaspoon nutmeg

½ teaspoon salt

4 tablespoons cold margarine

½ cup pecans

3 to 4 large, tart baking apples, sliced, with or without peel

1 teaspoon lemon juice

. . . .

Try this recipe with pears or peaches!

Preheat the oven to 350 degrees. Lightly grease an 8 × 8-inch baking dish with margarine or oil.

In a medium bowl, combine flour, oats, ¼ cup sugar, cinnamon, nutmeg and salt. With a pastry blender, your fingers or the back of a fork, cut in margarine until mixture is crumbly. Stir in pecans.

Fill baking dish with sliced apples. Sprinkle with remaining ½ cup sugar and lemon juice and cover with flour mixture. Bake for 20 to 25 minutes, until apples are easily pierced with a fork and topping is browned. Let crisp cool for 25 minutes before serving. Store leftover crisp covered in the fridge.

Yield: 6 SERVINGS

Prep time: 25 MINUTES

Difficulty:

CHOCOLATE STRAWBERRY TART

What's tastier than chocolate and strawberries? This tart has a crisp chocolate crunch and a creamy strawberry filling. It's a simple treat that is easy to throw together and even easier to dress up for special occasions.

CRUST:

1 cup flour

⅓ cup baking cocoa

¾ teaspoon salt

½ cup margarine, softened

¼ cup sugar

¼ cup yogurt

1 teaspoon vanilla

1 tablespoon milk

FILLING:

½ cup sugar

¼ cup cornstarch

1 bag frozen strawberries

½ cup water

2 cups sliced fresh strawberries, for garnish

For Crust: Combine flour, cocoa and salt in a small bowl. In a large bowl, cream together margarine and sugar until smooth. Add yogurt, vanilla and milk and stir until combined. Add flour mixture to yogurt mixture in three batches, mixing after each addition. Flatten dough into a disc, wrap in plastic wrap and refrigerate for at least 30 minutes, or until chilled.

Preheat the oven to 350 degrees. Lightly grease a 9-inch tart pan or other springform pan.

Roll out dough between two floured pieces of waxed paper until it is about ¼-inch thick. Press dough into the prepared pan and prick the bottom of it with a fork in several places to keep it from rising. This is a forgiving dough, so if it comes apart, just push it back together. Bake until firm, about 18 to 20 minutes. Let crust cool completely in the pan on a cooling rack. While crust is cooling, prepare filling.

For Filling: Combine sugar and cornstarch in a small saucepan. Add frozen strawberries and water. Bring contents to a boil, stirring constantly. Lower temperature and simmer, stirring constantly, for about 5 minutes or until thick. Remove from heat and stir mixture every few minutes until completely cool. Pour filling into cooled crust and decorate with fresh strawberries. Garnish with chocolate shavings or half a recipe of Chocolate Frosting (page 156), piped on decoratively. Store leftover tart covered in the fridge.

Yield: 1 TART, ABOUT 10 SLICES
Prep time: 35 MINUTES
Difficulty:

LEMON ALMOND TORTE

This is one of the fanciest treats in this book, and the most likely to combat scurvy! This is a cake that everyone will like, especially lemon-meringue lovers. It takes a bit of time to make, but the torte holds up beautifully in the refrigerator, so don't be afraid to make it the night before; just make sure it is sealed well in your fridge.

BASE:

1⅔ cups flour

⅓ cup almond meal or ground almonds

½ cup plus 2 tablespoons yogurt (1 6-ounce container)

½ cup sugar

½ cup brown sugar

½ cup margarine, melted and cooled

1 teaspoon vanilla

½ cup milk

FILLING:

¼ cup flour

1⅓ cups sugar

¼ cup cornstarch

1¾ cups water

pinch of salt

1 tablespoon lemon zest

¾ cup lemon juice

1 teaspoon peeled, grated fresh ginger

fresh raspberries (optional)

sliced almonds (optional)

. . . .

Top the base of the filling from Lime Coconut Bars (page 49) to make a Lime Torte!

. . . .

To make almond meal, process chopped almonds in a food processor until finely ground.

Preheat the oven to 350 degrees. Lightly grease and flour an 8- or 9-inch springform pan.

For Base: In a large bowl, combine flour and almond meal. In a medium bowl, cream together margarine, sugar and brown sugar. Stir in vanilla and yogurt. Add wet ingredients to dry ingredients and combine. Once mixed, stir in milk.

Spread dough in the bottom of the prepared pan, spreading up the sides of the pan to create a lip. Poke bottom of base with a fork in several places. Bake for 10 minutes, remove the pan and, using the back of a spoon or spatula, push down dough that has risen in the center of base. Continue baking for 15 more minutes, or until edge is slightly browned and toothpick comes out clean. Push down center of cake again and let cool on a rack. While the base is baking, begin preparing the lemon filling.

For Filling: In a medium saucepan, combine flour, sugar, cornstarch and salt. Whisk in water. Bring to a boil over medium heat, stirring constantly. Lower heat and whisk until thickened, approximately 5 minutes. Whisk in lemon zest, lemon juice and ginger. Continue mixing for 2 to 3 minutes, until mixture bubbles in the center. Remove from heat and pour into a bowl. Let sit, stirring occasionally, until cooled.

Pour filling into cooled base and decorate with raspberries and almond slices, if using. Refrigerate until set, at least 2 hours. Store leftover torte covered in fridge.

Yield: 1 TORTE, ABOUT 14 SLICES
Prep time: 1 HOUR
Difficulty:

CHOCOLATE WALNUT TOFFEE TART

This tart is chocolatey, gooey, carmelly and chewy. The walnuts and chocolate chips combine with the filling to create a simple, elegant tart that is a cinch to throw together but is very impressive. You know how rare anything with caramel is in the world of vegan baking, so what are you waiting for? Get to it!

CRUST:

1 cup flour

¼ cup baking cocoa, sifted

½ cup margarine, softened

½ cup sugar

FILLING:

1 cup brown sugar

¼ cup cornstarch

¼ cup flour

½ cup corn syrup or brown rice syrup

¼ cup milk

1 tablespoon oil

2 teaspoons molasses

1 teaspoon vanilla

¼ teaspoon maple extract

1 cup chocolate chips

1½ cups walnuts

sprinkle of sea salt

Preheat the oven to 350 degrees. Lightly grease a 10-inch tart pan or a 9-inch pie dish.

For Crust: In a small bowl, combine flour and cocoa. In a medium bowl, cream together margarine and sugar. Add dry ingredients to wet ingredients and mix until well-combined. Press dough into the prepared tart pan or pie dish. Bake for 12 minutes. Remove from oven and set on a cooling rack.

For Filling: While crust is baking, combine brown sugar, cornstarch and flour in a bowl. Mix well to avoid any clumps. Add corn syrup or brown rice syrup, milk, oil, molasses, vanilla and maple extract. Stir well, until mixture is thick and everything is incorporated. Fold in chocolate chips and walnuts and mix until they are coated with the caramel mixture. Pour filling into crust and top with a little sprinkle of sea salt. Bake for 25 minutes, until mixture bubbles. Remove from the oven and let cool on a rack for at least 30 minutes before serving. Store leftover tart covered at room temperature.

Yield: 1 TART, 10 TO 12 SLICES

Prep Time: 30 MINUTES

Difficulty:

PASTRIES

Mmm...pastries. Pastries can be a little more time consuming than, say, muffins, but they are always worth the effort. Flaky and buttery, a pastry with a cup of hot coffee goes a long way in getting your day (or afternoon…or evening…) off on the right foot. These recipes run the gamut from super simple to patisserie perfection. Whichever way you go, your tummy will say, "*Oui, oui!*"

- PUFF PASTRY
- PECAN PIE BITES
- STRAWBERRY CREAM PIE PUFFS
- SWEET CREAM APPLE STRUDEL
- POPPIN' POPOVERS
- PAIN AU CHOCOLAT
- GRANDMA T'S NUT ROLLS
- DELECTABLE DANISH
- BAKED CHOCOLATE-GLAZED DONUTS

PUFF PASTRY

Why would you make puff pastry from scratch when you can just buy it? Why do we make anything from scratch? Because we can, and because it always tastes better that way. This recipe is a little time consuming, but really other than having a lot of resting periods, it's not actually that difficult.

2 cups flour

1 teaspoon salt

1 tablespoon margarine, melted

½ cup water

¾ cup margarine (1½ sticks), at room temperature

. . . .

If you prep the dough for a recipe and you think the margarine may have warmed up, pop the prepared dough into the fridge or freezer for a few minutes to chill the margarine.

In the bowl of a food processor, if using, sift flour with salt. Add water and melted margarine and process until dough is smooth and elastic, about 1 minute.

If not using a food processor, sift flour with salt in a medium bowl. Make a well in the flour mixture and add melted margarine and water. Mix with a spatula to start and then begin gently kneading dough until all flour is incorporated.

On a clean, floured surface, roll out dough into a 9 x 18-inch rectangle. Between two pieces of waxed paper, roll room-temperature margarine into a 6 x 9-inch rectangle. Peel back the top sheet of the waxed paper and flip margarine rectangle over onto the middle of the dough rectangle (the 9-inch side of the margarine should be going the same direction as the 9-inch side of the dough). Fold both exposed "wings" of dough over margarine in thirds, like you are folding a letter. Rotate dough 90 degrees. Roll out dough into a 9 x 18-inch rectangle again. Fold dough into thirds again. Rotate dough 90 degrees and repeat. Let dough rest in the fridge for 2 hours.

Remove chilled dough from the fridge. Roll out dough into a 9 x 18-inch rectangle, fold into thirds and rotate 90 degrees. Repeat the process two more times. Let dough rest in the fridge again for 2 hours. If you want to store the dough for longer than 48 hours, you can freeze it at this point for up to 2 weeks. To use after freezing, let the dough thaw to fridge temperature and then pick up recipe with the next step.

Repeat the process of rolling dough out and folding into thirds two more times. This process creates many thin, buttery layers that will puff when you bake the dough. Let rest for 2 more hours.

At this point you can use the dough in any recipe calling for puff pastry. For the best puff possible, you want the dough to be cold. If the margarine is cold, the shock of the hot oven will cause the liquid in the margarine to evaporate, creating the puffy air pockets we are aiming for. Store unused pastry wrapped well in plastic wrap and a freezer bag in the freezer. Let pastry thaw to fridge temperature before using.

Yield: 1 SHEET OF PUFF PASTRY

Prep time: 1 HOUR ACTIVE, 5 HOURS INACTIVE

Difficulty:

PECAN PIE BITES

I love chocolatey, gooey pecan pie, and when I want it in a rush, these bites hit the spot. Let them sit for at least 20 minutes after baking to let the filling set. Try them à la mode with your favorite vanilla soy or rice ice cream.

6 5 x 5-inch squares puff pastry, thawed

2 tablespoons melted margarine, divided

⅓ cup brown sugar, packed

2 tablespoons cornstarch

1 tablespoon maple syrup

⅔ cup chopped pecans

⅓ cup chocolate chips

1 tablespoon blackstrap molasses

1 teaspoon vanilla

¼ teaspoon salt

Preheat the oven to 350 degrees.

Brush tops of puff pastry squares with 1 tablespoon melted margarine. Place them into jumbo muffin cups, dry side touching the tin, creating a shell. In a large bowl, mix brown sugar and cornstarch until well-combined. Stir in pecans and chocolate chips. Add maple syrup, molasses, vanilla, remaining 1 tablespoon margarine and salt and combine until mixture is thick and ingredients are well-incorporated.

Spoon mixture evenly among the muffin cups. Bake for 9 to 11 minutes or until puff pastry is puffed and browned. Remove from the oven and let cool for 15 minutes before serving. Store leftover bites covered at room temperature.

Yield: 6 BITES
Prep time: 20 MINUTES
Difficulty: 🥄

Strawberry Cream Pie Puffs

These sweet little pies are great for dessert or for a devilishly sweet breakfast with coffee. If you've taken the plunge and made the puff pastry recipe, this is a great way to try it out. If not, there's always Pepperidge Farms' puff pastry—accidentally vegan!

4 5 x 5-inch squares puff pastry
2 tablespoons sugar
½ cup strawberry jam
¼ cup soy cream cheese
1 tablespoon margarine, melted
White Icing (page 155)

Preheat the oven to 350 degrees. Line a baking sheet with parchment paper.

In the center of each square of puff pastry, spread 1 tablespoon cream cheese and sprinkle ½ tablespoon sugar. Top each square with 2 tablespoons jam. Fold pastries corner to corner to make triangles. Seal edges using a little bit of water and pinch them well. Poke a hole with a knife on the top of each one to help vent the pastries.

Place pies on the prepared baking sheet about 2 inches apart and bake for 10 to 12 minutes or until puffy and lightly browned. Let cool slightly, then brush the tops with margarine to soften them. Drizzle with icing. Store leftover pies covered in the fridge.

Yield: 4 PIES
Prep time: 15 MINUTES
Difficulty:

Sweet Cream Apple Strudel

This treat is so delicious, it's hard to eat just one slice. The creamy filling and tart apples combine with the flaky, buttery crust to make the ultimate breakfast pastry. You can always split the pastry in half to make two smaller strudels. The reason we keep putting the pastry in the fridge between steps is to keep it chilled so that it truly puffs up in the oven.

1 recipe puff pastry, thawed to fridge temperature

½ an 8-ounce container of soy cream cheese

¼ plus ⅓ cup sugar, divided

½ teaspoon vanilla

⅓ cup sugar

2 tablespoons cornstarch

1 teaspoon cinnamon

3 tart apples, peeled and sliced into ½-inch slices

sugar to sprinkle

Preheat the oven to 375 degrees. Line a large baking sheet with parchment paper. Roll out puff pastry to fit the pan, then return it to the fridge.

In a small bowl, combine cream cheese, ¼ cup sugar and vanilla. Mix well. Bring puff pastry out of fridge and set baking sheet on the counter so the shorter, 16-inch side of the puff pastry is perpendicular to you. Spread the cream cheese mixture down the middle of the puff pastry, leaving 1½ inches on either edge, then return to the fridge. Combine remaining ⅓ cup sugar, cornstarch and cinnamon in a bowl. Add the apples and toss to coat. Remove puff pastry from fridge. Place apple mixture on top of the cream cheese mixture, scraping out any remaining sugar mixture onto the apples. Fold the short 1½-inch edges in and fold one long side over the other to cover the apples. Your pastry should now look like a log. You may need to use a little water to seal the edges of the pastry.

With a sharp knife, score several lines through the top of the strudel log all the way down to the apples. Brush the top of the log with water and sprinkle on a little sugar. Bake for 25 to 30 minutes or until golden and puffy. Let cool for at least 30 minutes before serving. Store leftover strudel covered in fridge.

Yield: 8 SERVINGS
Prep time: 20 MINUTES
Difficulty: 🥢🥢

POPPIN' POPOVERS

Popovers are a very popular bread side dish in Minnesota. They are the American answer to Yorkshire Pudding, with a crusty outer shell and slightly eggy filling. The unique cooking method creates instant heat in the middle of the dough, which makes large air pockets that become crispy on the outside. These are great with a thick soup, but they also make a delicious breakfast with a pat of margarine and some jam.

6 teaspoons margarine, chilled

1 cup flour

½ teaspoon baking powder

¼ teaspoon salt

½ package silken tofu, medium or firm

1 cup milk

1 teaspoon melted margarine

Preheat the oven to 425 degrees. Lightly grease the bottoms of 6 regular-sized muffin cups with oil or margarine. Place 1 teaspoon margarine in the bottom of each cup.

In the bowl of a food processor or in a large bowl, combine flour, baking powder, salt, tofu, milk and melted margarine. Process on high or blend vigorously with electric hand beaters until everything is incorporated and mixture is smooth. Place muffin tin in the oven for 1 minute to heat the pan and melt the margarine. Remove from oven and quickly divide the batter into the muffin cups, using a ¼-cup measuring cup.

Bake for 20 minutes at 425 degrees then reduce the oven temperature to 325 degrees. Bake until popovers are dark golden and crisp. Let cool for 15 minutes in the muffin tin before serving or turning out onto a cooling rack to finish cooling. Store leftover popovers covered in the fridge.

Yield: 6 POPOVERS
Prep time: 15 MINUTES
Difficulty:

Pain au Chocolat

This recipe will put your baking skills to the test, but your chocolate-filled croissants will be so delicate and delicious that you will feel pretty darn proud and your friends and family will be in awe of your mad baking skills. Pain au Chocolat are actually not as hard to make as you may fear, but they require a little time, patience and love. Beware that many vegan margarines can be salty, so you'll want to use one with the lowest sodium that you can find.

1¼-ounce packet (2¼ teaspoons) rapid-rise yeast

¼ cup warm water

1 teaspoon sugar

2½ cups flour

⅛ teaspoon salt

¾ cup milk

¾ cup plus 2 tablespoons margarine, room temperature, divided

¾ cup bittersweet or semi-sweet chocolate, coarsely chopped

1 tablespoon margarine, melted

In a large bowl, combine yeast, water and sugar. Let sit for about 5 minutes, until foamy. Add 1 cup flour, salt and milk and stir to combine. Continue incorporating flour in ½-cup increments until a dough forms. Turn out onto a floured surface and lightly knead for about 2 to 3 minutes, until dough is no longer sticky. It does not need to be smooth and elastic like bread dough does.

Roll out dough into an 18 x 12-inch rectangle. Visually divide the dough into thirds that are 6 x 12 inches. Spread half of the room-temperature margarine evenly onto the middle third of the rectangle. Fold the right third over onto the margarine-covered third and spread the remaining margarine on the section that is now on top. Fold remaining left third on top of the second margarine-covered third. You should now have a rectangle of dough that is approximately 6 x 12 inches and has two layers of margarine-covered dough inside it. Roll out dough into another 18 x 12-inch rectangle. Visually divide the dough into fourths and fold the outer fourths in so the edges of the dough halves are touching in the middle, to roughly make a square. Fold one of these dough halves onto the other, so there are four dough layers stacked on top of each other. Wrap dough in plastic and refrigerate for 2 hours.

Line a baking sheet with parchment paper. Remove dough from the refrigerator and roll out into a 12 x 16-inch rectangle. Cut dough into 12 3 x 4-inch rectangles. On the short end of each small rectangle, about ½ inch from the edge, sprinkle about 1 tablespoon of the chocolate onto the dough. Roll dough up into a fat cylinder and slightly flatten it, seam side down, onto the baking sheet. You may need to poke pieces of chocolate back into the ends of the pastry. Repeat with remaining pieces of dough, placing pastries about 3 inches apart on the baking sheet. Cover pastries and let rise until doubled in size, about 1 ½ to 2 hours.

Preheat oven to 400 degrees. Gently brush the tops of each pastry with melted margarine and sprinkle with sugar, if desired. Bake for 15 to 18 minutes or until puffy and lightly browned. Let cool on the sheet for at least 20 minutes before serving. Store leftover pastries covered at room temperature.

Yield: 12 PAIN AU CHOCOLAT
Prep time: 50 MINUTES ACTIVE
Difficulty:

GRANDMA T'S NUT ROLLS

My grandmother made these rolls every year for the holidays and froze them in bulk, so there was always one ready to eat. Once the family started migrating around the country, she sometimes sent her treats out a couple weeks before Christmas. While the original recipe calls for three eggs, I feel that this vegan recipe is just as good, with an even more pastry-like crust. You could always make a thin White Icing (page 155) to glaze the rolls, but we grew up eating them plain.

DOUGH:

1 packet (¼ ounce or 2¼ teaspoons) active yeast

¼ cup warm water

½ cup margarine, softened

3 tablespoons sugar

3 tablespoons ground flaxseed

½ cup plus 2 tablespoons yogurt (1 6-ounce container)

3 cups flour

FILLING:

2 cups chopped walnuts

1 cup sugar

2 cups raisins

1½ teaspoons vanilla

¼ cup milk

For Dough: In a small bowl, stir yeast and a pinch of sugar into water until yeast dissolves. Let sit for about 5 minutes, or until foamy.

In a large bowl, cream together margarine and sugar. Add flaxseed and yogurt and blend with an electric hand mixer for 3 minutes, until mixture is creamy and flaxseed is softened. Add yeast mixture and blend until mixed. Add 1½ cups flour and mix until well-incorporated. Continue adding flour ½ cup at a time until a soft dough comes together (you may not use all the flour). Turn dough out onto a floured surface and knead well for 3 to 5 minutes, adding more flour if necessary. Dough should be soft and slightly tacky.

For Filling: In a small bowl, combine walnuts, sugar, raisins, vanilla and milk.

For Assembly: Line a baking sheet with parchment paper. Divide dough into three parts. Roll each piece out into a 10 x 12-inch rectangle. Divide filling among the three rectangles and spread it out, leaving a ½-inch border on two opposite sides of each rectangle. Starting with one of those sides, roll the dough into a log, creating a spiral on the side. Pinch the ends and smooth the seams. Repeat with other two rectangles of dough. Place nut rolls seam-side down on the prepared baking sheet. Cover with a kitchen towel and let rise at room temperature for at least 1 hour.

Preheat the oven to 350 degrees. Bake nut rolls for 25 to 30 minutes or until tops are browned. Remove rolls from the oven and brush with margarine. Cool on the baking sheet on a cooling rack. Store leftover rolls wrapped in plastic in the fridge, or freeze for up to 1 month.

Yield: 3 ROLLS, 8 SLICES EACH
Prep time: 40 MINUTES ACTIVE
Difficulty: 🥄🥄🥄

DELECTABLE DANISH

Making Danish is time consuming, so plan this for a day when you're going to be lounging around and can tend to it every few hours. Or start the night before, prolong the refrigeration time and get up a little early to treat brunch eaters to some fresh pastries. You can fill the Danish with any kind of preserves or pie filling you'd like—I love apple or raspberry.

1 packet (¼ ounce or 2¼ teaspoons) active dry yeast

¼ cup warm water

¼ cup margarine, softened

¼ cup sugar

½ teaspoon salt

2 cups flour

1 teaspoon cinnamon

½ cup milk

2 tablespoons ground flaxseed

1 stick (½ cup) cold margarine, thinly sliced

preserves or pie filling of your choice

1 recipe White Icing (page 155)

In a small bowl, dissolve yeast in warm water with a pinch of sugar. Let sit about 5 minutes, or until foamy.

In a separate bowl, cream together margarine, sugar and salt. Add ½ cup flour, cinnamon and milk. Add flaxseed and beat with an electric hand mixer for about 2 minutes. Add yeast mixture and mix well. Add additional flour in batches until a soft dough comes together. Cover bowl with a kitchen towel and let dough rise at room temperature until it doubles in size, about 2 hours. Place covered bowl in refrigerator for 3 hours.

Line a baking sheet with parchment paper and set aside. Turn out dough onto a lightly floured surface.

Roll out dough into a large rectangle, about 12 x 15 inches. Place half of the cold, thin margarine slices (about 15 to 20) evenly onto the dough. Fold dough in thirds, and roll out into another 12 x 15-inch rectangle. Place the remaining half of the margarine slices evenly over the dough. Fold dough into thirds again and roll out into a 9 x 12-inch rectangle. Cut dough into 12 3 x 3-inch squares. Fold the corners of each square into the middle and press down with the back of a spoon to secure corners and make an indentation. Cover with a kitchen towel and let rise in a warm place until doubled in size, about 1 hour.

Preheat the oven to 375 degrees. Press down any loose corners of the squares and fill centers with a scoop of preserves or pie filling.

Bake for 10 to 12 minutes or until lightly browned. Remove from pan to cool on a rack. Brush with melted margarine. Once Danish are cooled, drizzle with White Icing. Store leftover Danish covered in fridge.

Yield: 12 DANISH
Prep time: 1 HOUR ACTIVE, 5 TO 6 HOURS INACTIVE
Difficulty:

Baked Chocolate-Glazed Donuts

These donuts are baked, so they are a little less dense than their fried counterparts, but they are very easy and delicious! If you don't have a donut pan (because besides Martha Stewart and me, who really does?), feel free to roll them into small balls and bake them in a mini-muffin tin to make donut holes.

1¼ cups flour

⅓ cup baking cocoa

½ teaspoon salt

¼ cup sugar

½ cup margarine, softened

¼ cup unsweetened applesauce

½ cup milk

1 teaspoon vanilla

1 recipe White Icing (page 155)

Preheat the oven to 350 degrees. Lightly grease 6-cup donut pan or a 12-cup mini-muffin tin with margarine or oil.

In a medium bowl, combine flour, cocoa and salt. In a large bowl, cream together sugar and margarine. Add the applesauce, milk and vanilla and stir until well-incorporated. Add dry ingredients to wet ingredients in two batches and mix until well-combined.

Spoon mixture evenly into prepared donut pan or mini-muffin tin. Bake for 12 to 15 minutes (7 to 8 minutes if using mini-muffin tin) or until tops are set and a toothpick comes out clean. Let donuts cool completely before drizzling with White Icing. Store leftover donuts covered at room temperature.

Yield: 6 DONUTS OR 12 DONUT HOLES

Prep time: 20 MINUTES

Difficulty:

YEASTED TREATS

Many people are afraid to work with yeast, but if you start out with something easy like a pizza crust, you'll be making bread in no time. The first few times you make bread, I recommend using all-purpose flour. It's easy to work with while you're getting a feel for the process. With that experience under your belt, you can then venture on to using blends of whole-grain flours.

All of these recipes are made by hand—no bread machines here! I'm sure that you could find appropriate settings on your bread machine if that's what you prefer, but making bread is not scary or hard, so try it without the newfangled gadgetry! I like to be really hands-on when I'm making food, especially something as mysterious as yeasted breads. Turn on some music and start kneading! You've never felt accomplishment in the kitchen until you've made a loaf of bread. So enjoy! It's a fun ride.

- BETTER-THAN BREADSTICKS
- HERBED PIZZA DOUGH
- BASIC WHEATY BREAD
- EZEKIEL BREAD
- ROASTED GARLIC OLIVE LOAF
- ROSEMARY FOCACCIA
- GOIN' UP NORTH LOAF
- SWEET WHEAT ROLLS
- GARLIC ROLLS
- BRAIDED HOLIDAY BREAD
- KLARY'S SUKERBOLEN (SUGAR BREAD)
- DESSERT PIZZA

BETTER-THAN BREADSTICKS

There is a certain Italian chain restaurant that I'm sure you all know, but which will remain nameless, that is quite popular for its breadsticks. Back in the day, I too loved them and would eat them by the basket. After one particularly bad craving, I came up with these breadsticks to satisfy myself, and wow, they are good. They are soft in the middle, with a hint of garlic, and buttery and salty on the outside. The only thing better than how delicious they are is how easy this recipe is. It's a beautiful thing.

½ packet (⅛ ounce or 1⅛ teaspoon)
rapid-rise yeast
¼ teaspoon sugar
½ plus 1 tablespoon warm water
1½ cups flour
½ teaspoon powdered garlic
2 teaspoons olive oil
1 tablespoon margarine, melted
sea salt, for sprinkling

In a large bowl, combine yeast, sugar and 1 tablespoon warm water. Let sit for about 5 minutes, or until foamy. In a separate bowl, combine flour and powdered garlic. Add remaining ½ cup water and oil to yeast mixture and begin to incorporate flour mixture ½ cup at a time until a sticky dough forms. Turn dough out onto a floured surface and knead for about 5 minutes, until it becomes smooth and elastic, adding flour as needed. Dough should be moist and tacky, but not sticky. Place dough in an oiled bowl, turning once to coat. Cover with a kitchen towel and let rise in a warm place until doubled in size, about 45 minutes.

Line a baking sheet with parchment paper. Punch down dough to deflate and turn out onto a floured surface. Divide dough in half, then divide each half into 3 evenly sized balls. Roll out each ball into a stick about 7 inches long. Place sticks on the baking sheet about 1½ inches apart. Cover and let rise for 20 minutes.

Preheat the oven to 400 degrees. Bake for 12 to 15 minutes or until breadsticks are lightly browned. Remove from the oven and let cool for 5 minutes before brushing on melted margarine. Sprinkle with sea salt and serve warm. Store leftover breadsticks covered in the fridge.

Yield: 6 BREADSTICKS
Prep time: 25 MINUTES ACTIVE
Difficulty:

HERBED PIZZA DOUGH

This recipe makes one large, thick pizza crust. Check out my blog for my prized Pesto Tofu Ricotta recipe, a sure hit with every bite. Dress it up with your favorite toppings and be nice—pizza was meant for sharing!

1 packet (¼ ounce or 2¼ teaspoons) active dry yeast

1 teaspoon sugar

¾ cup warm water

2 cups flour

½ teaspoon salt

2 teaspoon Italian spice, or 1 teaspoon oregano mixed with 1 large pinch each rosemary, sage and thyme

2 tablespoons olive oil

. . . .

Pizza stones are inexpensive and will forever change the way you eat homemade pizza.

In a small bowl, combine yeast, sugar and warm water. Let sit for 5 minutes, or until foamy. In another bowl, sift together flour, salt and herbs. Add yeast mixture and oil to flour mixture and stir with a spatula until combined. Turn dough out onto a floured surface and knead for about 5 minutes, or until smooth and elastic, adding more flour as needed. Place in an oiled bowl and turn to coat. Cover with a kitchen towel and let rise in a warm place for an hour, or until doubled in size.

Turn dough out onto a lightly floured surface. Roll out with a rolling pin or push with your hands to get crust to desired thickness. The dough may resist your efforts, but if you are gentle yet firm, it will stretch out.

Preheat the oven to 450 degrees if using a pizza pan; preheat the oven to 500 degrees if using a pizza stone.

Lay dough on a pizza pan, or parchment paper if using a pizza stone, sprinkled with a little flour or cornmeal and top with your favorite sauce and toppings. If using a pizza pan, bake at 450 degrees for 15 to 20 minutes, or until bottom of crust is browned and bread sounds hollow when tapped with a spoon. If baking on a pizza stone (which I can't recommend highly enough), bake at 500 degrees for 7 to 9 minutes, or until bottom of crust is browned. Store leftover pizza covered in the fridge.

Yield: 1 PIZZA, 8 SLICES
Prep time: 20 MINUTES ACTIVE
Difficulty:

BASIC WHEATY BREAD

This bread is not a whole-wheat bread, but rather it has a blend of white-wheat and all-purpose flours. It's much more substantial than white bread, and it's also easier to make than straight-up wheat bread.

1 cup warm water

1 tablespooon sugar

1 packet (¼ ounce or 2¼ teaspoons) active dry yeast

2 cups white-wheat flour

1 cup all-purpose flour

1 teaspoon salt

3 tablespoons oil

In a large bowl, combine water, sugar and yeast. Let sit for 5 minutes or until foamy. In a small bowl, combine white-wheat flour, all-purpose flour and salt.

Add 1½ cups flour mixture to yeast mixture. Once combined, add oil. Continue adding flour mixture ½ cup at a time until a nice sticky dough forms. Turn dough out onto a lightly floured surface and knead for about 5 minutes, or until smooth and elastic. Cover the bowl with a kitchen towel and let dough rise in a warm place until doubled in size, about 1 hour.

When dough has risen, punch it down, turn it out onto a lightly floured surface and gently knead for about a minute, until the dough is soft and elastic again. At this point you have two options: You can make a loaf in a pan or make a bakery-style round. For a loaf, lightly grease a 9 x 5-inch loaf pan. Shape dough by rolling it out a little and then rolling it up to fit the pan, tucking in the ends. For a bakery-style round, shape dough into an oval and place on a baking sheet lined with parchment paper.

Cover dough and let rise again until doubled in size, about 40 minutes. Preheat the oven to 375 degrees. Bake for 30 to 35 minutes if using a loaf pan, or 22 to 27 for a bakery-style round, or until bread is nicely browned and sounds hollow when tapped with a spoon. Let cool in the pan. Brush on oil or melted butter while bread is still warm to make the top crust softer. Store leftover bread covered at room temperature.

Yield: 10 SLICES
Prep time: 30 MINUTES ACTIVE
Difficulty:

EZEKIEL BREAD

This moist, dense loaf makes fantastic toast bread and will leave you feeling very satisfied and full for hours after breakfast. You can also serve it up with a hearty bowl of soup. It is full of different grains and legumes and packs a powerful nutritional punch.

1¼ cups warm water

1 packet (¼ ounce or 2¼ teaspoons) active dry yeast

1 teaspoon sugar

1 cup all-purpose flour

1 cup white whole-wheat flour

1 cup barley flour or spelt flour

½ cup chickpea flour

¼ cup cooked lentils (brown or red work best)

2 tablespoons oil

½ teaspoon salt

1 tablespoon blackstrap molasses

In a large bowl, combine warm water, yeast and sugar. Let sit for about 5 minutes, or until foamy. In a medium bowl, combine all-purpose flour, white whole-wheat flour, barley flour and chickpea flour.

In a separate bowl, mash lentils with a large fork or potato masher. Add lentils to yeast mixture along with oil, salt and molasses and stir to combine. Add flour mixture to lentil mixture one cup at a time, stirring to incorporate after each addition. When dough is formed, turn out onto a lightly floured surface and knead until smooth, about 6 minutes. Place dough in a lightly oiled bowl and turn to coat. Cover with a kitchen towel and let rise in a warm place for about 1 hour.

Punch dough down and turn out onto a lightly floured surface. Knead lightly and shape into a loaf by flattening slightly and then rolling into a tight roll that is 8 to 9 inches long. Place in a lightly greased 9 × 5-inch loaf pan. Cover and let rise until loaf is doubled and arches above the edge of the pan (about 45 minutes).

Preheat oven to 375 degrees. Bake for 50 to 60 minutes or until loaf sounds hollow when tapped with a spoon. Cool in pan. For a softer crust, brush oil or melted margarine on top while bread is warm. Store leftover bread covered at room temperature.

Yield: 1 LOAF, 10 SLICES
Prep time: 30 MINUTES ACTIVE
Difficulty:

Roasted Garlic Olive Loaf

The garlic in this recipe caramelizes and becomes sweet while baking and contrasts with the salty tang of the olives, making for an irresistible loaf of bread.

½ packet (⅛ ounce or 1⅛ teaspoon) rapid-rise yeast

¼ cup plus ⅓ cup warm water, divided

pinch of sugar

1 cup all-purpose flour

1 cup whole-wheat flour

¼ teaspoon salt

1½ tablespoons olive oil

½ head of garlic, peeled and roughly chopped into large chunks

¼ cup kalamata olives, well drained and roughly chopped

In a large bowl, combine yeast with ¼ cup warm water and sugar. Let sit until thick and frothy, about 5 minutes. In another bowl, combine all-purpose flour, whole-wheat flour and salt. Add remaining ⅓ cup water and olive oil to yeast mixture and begin incorporating flour ½ cup at a time until a sticky dough forms. Add garlic and kalamata olives and turn dough out onto a floured surface. Continue incorporating flour until dough is moist but no longer sticky to the touch. Knead for about 5 to 8 minutes, or until elastic and smooth. Put dough in an oiled bowl and turn once to coat. Cover with a kitchen towel and let rise in a warm place until doubled in size, about an hour.

Once dough has risen, turn out onto a floured surface and lightly knead. Shape into a round loaf and put on a floured baking sheet and let rise again until doubled in size, about 30 minutes. You can also bake the dough in a loaf pan, rather than shaping it into a round, by rolling out dough into a rectangle and rolling it up tightly into a log; then shape into a loaf and put into a greased loaf pan and let rise again until doubled in size, about 30 minutes.

While loaf is on its second rise, preheat the oven to 350 degrees. Bake for 30 minutes or until bread is browned and sounds hollow when tapped with a spoon. Remove from the oven and let sit for 5 minutes. Brush top of loaf with olive oil or melted margarine. Let cool for 20 minutes before serving. Store leftover bread covered at room temperature.

Yield: 1 LOAF, ABOUT 8 SLICES
Prep time: 20 MINUTES ACTIVE
Difficulty: 🥄🥄

ROSEMARY FOCACCIA

This bread is easy to make and is wonderful with pasta or soup or for making a sandwich. Play with topping ideas such as tomato slices, olives or red onions. Everything tastes good with focaccia!

DOUGH:

1 packet (¼ ounce or 2¼ teaspoons) active dry yeast

1 teaspoon sugar

1¾ cups lukewarm water

1 teaspoon salt

2 tablespoons olive oil

4 to 4½ cups flour

1 teaspoon finely chopped fresh rosemary or 1½ teaspoons dried rosemary

TOPPING:

1 to 1½ tablespoons olive oil

2 teaspoons finely chopped fresh rosemary or 1½ teaspoons dried rosemary

1½ teaspoons coarse salt, or to taste

For Dough: In a large bowl, gently stir together yeast, sugar and water and let sit for 5 minutes or until foamy. Stir in salt and olive oil. Add flour 1 cup at a time and knead dough, adding as much flour as necessary to form a soft, slightly sticky dough. Turn dough out onto a floured surface and knead for about 4 minutes, until dough is elastic and smooth. Place dough in a lightly oiled bowl and turn to coat. Cover with a kitchen towel and let rise in a warm place for 1 hour, or until doubled in size.

Grease a jelly-roll pan or two 8-inch cake pans with margarine or oil. Once dough has risen, punch it down, then knead in rosemary and spread dough into the prepared pan. Shape the dough in each pan using your hands to create a disc. It does not need to touch the edges completely, as it will once it rises. Let it rise again, covered loosely with a kitchen towel, for 30 minutes.

Preheat the oven to 400 degrees.

For Topping: Brush on olive oil and sprinkle with sea salt and rosemary. Dimple the dough with your fingers, making ¼-inch-deep indentations.

Bake for 35 to 40 minutes, or until bread is golden. Let foccacia rest in the pan for 5 minutes before serving. Store leftover bread covered at room temperature.

Yield: 8 LARGE SLICES
Prep time: 25 MINUTES ACTIVE
Difficulty:

GOiN' UP NORTH LOAF

Minnesotans love their wild rice and really, what's not to love? It's fragrant, chewy and high in protein. In this loaf, wild rice adds a lovely texture and flavor that makes the bread delicious as a side, but also flavorful enough to enjoy on its own.

¼ teaspoon sugar

1¼ cups warm water, divided

1 packet (¼ ounce or 2¼ teaspoons) rapid-rise yeast

1 cup whole-wheat flour

2 to 2½ cups all-purpose flour

¼ teaspoon salt

1 tablespoon olive oil

1 cup cooked wild rice

. . . .

Replace the wild rice with cooked quinoa to make Protein Bread.

In a large bowl, sprinkle sugar into ¼ cup warm water. Add yeast and let sit for 5 minutes or until foamy. In a separate bowl, mix whole-wheat flour, all-purpose flour and salt. Add oil, remaining 1 cup water, wild rice and 2 cups flour mixture to yeast mixture. Continue adding flour and mix until a soft dough comes together. Turn dough out onto a floured surface and knead for 5 to 7 minutes, adding flour as needed, until dough becomes smooth and elastic. Place dough in an oiled bowl and turn to coat. Cover with a kitchen towel and let rise in a warm place for 1 hour.

Lightly grease a 9 x 5-inch loaf pan. Punch down dough and turn out on to a floured surface. Roll out dough into a 10 x 16-inch rectangle. Starting on the short end, tightly roll the dough into a cylinder, tuck the ends under and place dough in prepared loaf pan. Cover and let rise until the highest part of the dough is about 1 inch above the edge of the pan, about 30 to 45 minutes.

Preheat the oven to 375 degrees. Bake for 40 to 45 minutes, until loaf is browned and sounds hollow when tapped with a spoon. Let bread cool on a cooling rack for 15 minutes before brushing top of loaf with melted margarine, then continue to cool for an hour before removing from the pan. Store leftover bread covered at room temperature.

Yield: 1 LOAF, 10 TO 12 SLICES
Prep time: 25 MINUTES ACTIVE
Difficulty: 🥄🥄🥄

SWEET WHEAT ROLLS

These lightly sweetened wheat rolls are wonderful with soup, pasta or salad. I like to push a little margarine into the middle of them when they come out of the oven. They are very easy to make, are deliciously yeasty and have a cute presentation.

2 packets (½ ounce or 4½ teaspoons) active dry yeast

1 teaspoon sugar

1 cup warm water

2 cups whole-wheat flour

1 cup all-purpose flour

¼ cup margarine, softened

¼ cup agave nectar or maple syrup

1 tablespoon ground flaxseed

1 teaspoon salt

Combine yeast, sugar and warm water in large bowl. Let stand 5 minutes or until foamy. Combine whole-wheat flour and all-purpose flour in a medium bowl. Measure 1½ cups flour mixture into yeast mixture. Add margarine, agave nectar, flaxseed and salt. Beat with an electric hand mixer at low speed until smooth.

Add another 1 cup flour mixture to dough. You may need to do this by hand. Continue adding flour and mixing until dough is no longer sticky. Turn dough out onto a lightly floured surface. Knead for 5 to 8 minutes, or until dough is smooth and elastic. Place in a large, lightly oiled bowl and turn to coat. Cover with a kitchen towel and let rise in a warm place for about 1 hour or until doubled in size.

Preheat the oven to 375 degrees. Lightly grease 12 muffin cups with margarine or oil.

Punch down dough. Turn dough out onto a lightly floured surface and gently knead a few times. Divide dough into 12 equal pieces. Divide each piece into 3 small, smooth balls. Place 3 balls in each muffin cup. Cover and let rise for about 30 minutes, or until doubled in size.

Bake for 10 minutes or until rolls are golden brown. Rolls are best served warm. Store leftover rolls covered at room temperature.

Yield: 12 ROLLS
Prep time: 25 MINUTES ACTIVE
Difficulty: 🥄🥄

GARLIC ROLLS

The more you let them rise, the more versatile these supereasy rolls are. Let them rise a bit longer and higher for sandwich buns, or enjoy them a bit smaller as dinner rolls. The garlic cloves roast into the rolls while they're baking, making for a savory treat on each one. Delicious and pretty!

1 cup warm water

1 tablespoon sugar

1 packet (¼ ounce or 2¼ teaspoons) active dry yeast

1 tablespoon oil

½ teaspoon salt

2½ to 3 cups flour

2 heads of garlic, peeled

. . . .

These rolls taste incredible with a cheesy topping! Blend ¼ cup raw cashews, 2 tablespoons nutritional yeast and ½ teaspoon salt in a food processor until well ground. Brush warm rolls with oil or margarine and sprinkle topping on for a tasty treat. It's also good on popcorn!

In a large bowl, combine water, sugar and yeast. Let sit for 5 minutes, or until foamy. Add oil and salt. Stir in 1 cup flour, then continue incorporating flour ½ cup at a time, until a nice dough pulls together. Turn dough out onto a lightly floured surface and knead for about 5 minutes, or until dough is smooth and elastic. Place in an oiled bowl and turn to coat. Cover with a kitchen towel and let rise in a warm place until doubled in size, about 45 minutes.

Punch down dough and turn out onto floured surface. Knead lightly and divide dough into 12 equal parts. Roll each part until smooth and place about 2 inches apart on a baking sheet lined with parchment paper. Press a garlic clove into the top of each roll. Cover and let rise again for at least 30 minutes.

Preheat oven to 400 degrees. Bake for 12 to 15 minutes or until rolls are lightly browned and garlic cloves are soft and golden. Remove rolls from the oven and cool on the pan. Store leftover rolls covered at room temperature.

Yield: 12 ROLLS
Prep time: 25 MINUTES ACTIVE
Difficulty:

BRAIDED HOLIDAY BREAD

This bread is intoxicating: soft and moist with a nice, thin layer of icing on top. The fragrance of orange fills your head while you bite into sweet bursts of raisins and an occasional chunk of pecan. It makes a perfect holiday hostess gift, if it makes it out of your house in one piece!

¼ cup plus ⅓ cup warm water, divided

1 packet (¼ ounce or 2¼ teaspoons) rapid-rise yeast

½ cup sugar

2 tablespoons ground flaxseed

½ cup plus 1 tablespoon margarine, melted

¾ cup plus 2 tablespoons warm milk

1 teaspoon salt

4 to 5 cups flour

⅔ cup raisins

⅔ cup chopped pecans

zest of one orange

1 recipe White Icing (page 155)

In a large bowl, combine ¼ cup warm water, yeast and a pinch of sugar. Let sit for about 5 minutes, or until foamy. While yeast is sitting, in a small bowl, combine flaxseed and remaining ⅓ cup water. Whip mixture with a fork until it looks a bit cloudy and let sit for several minutes to thicken. In another bowl, combine sugar, margarine and milk. Add milk mixture and flaxseed mixture to yeast mixture. Beat until combined; it is easiest to use an electric hand mixer. Mix flour with salt and begin adding flour mixture to yeast mixture 1 cup at a time. As dough begins to thicken, you may wish to switch over to a spatula for mixing. Once a sticky dough comes together, add raisins, pecans and orange zest. Turn dough out onto a floured surface and knead, adding flour as needed, until dough is soft and elastic, but no longer sticky, about 8 to 10 minutes. Place dough in an oiled bowl, turning once to coat. Cover with a kitchen towel and let rise in a warm place until doubled in size, about 1 hour.

After dough has risen, line a baking sheet with parchment paper. Punch dough down and turn out onto a floured surface. Knead dough several times to make it more elastic again. Divide dough into three even pieces. Roll out each piece into a thick rope, approximately 18 to 20 inches long, making sure that all three are the same length. Lay pieces on the baking sheet and pinch together the three ends that are farthest from you. Begin to braid the bread, overlapping the dough strips until completely braided. Pinch together the braided ends well. Cover dough and let rise for about 20 minutes.

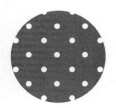

While dough is on its second rise, preheat the oven to 375 degrees. Once dough has risen, gently brush the top with remaining melted margarine and bake for 15 minutes at 375 degrees. Then reduce the heat to 350 degrees and continue baking for 20 minutes longer, until bread is browned and golden. Let loaf cool completely, then ice with White Icing. Store leftover bread covered at room temperature.

Yield: 1 LARGE LOAF, ABOUT 14 SLICES
Prep time: 40 MINUTES ACTIVE
Difficulty:

Klary's Sukerbolen (Sugar Bread)

A dear friend of mine who is a fellow lover of baking shared this traditional Dutch bread recipe with me. It was simple to veganize, and it beats the pants off of any cinnamon bread I've ever had. Rather than having a typical cinnamon swirl, this bread has delightfully crunchy cinnamon bites that sneak up on you.

3½ cups flour

2 packets (½ ounce or 4½ teaspoons) active dry yeast

1 teaspoon salt

⅛ teaspoon nutmeg

¾ cup plus 1 tablespoon warm milk

3 tablespoons maple syrup or agave nectar

¼ cup sugar

1 tablespoon ground flaxseed

3 tablespoons water

⅓ cup margarine, melted

1 tablespoon cinnamon

½ cup slightly crushed sugar cubes

In a medium bowl, mix flour, yeast, salt and nutmeg together. In a large bowl, mix milk, maple syrup and sugar together. In a small food processor or a separate bowl with an electric hand mixer, mix the flaxseed and water for about 2 minutes, or until gooey. Add flaxseed mixture to milk mixture, then add in the margarine. Add flour mixture starting with 2 cups of flour and continuing ½ cup at a time until a sticky dough pulls together. Turn dough out on a lightly floured surface and knead, incorporating more flour as necessary, until dough is smooth. Place dough in an oiled bowl, and turn to coat. Cover with a kitchen towel and let rise in a warm place for about 1 hour.

Lightly grease a 9 x 5-inch loaf pan with margarine or oil. In a small bowl, mix sugar cubes with cinnamon. Punch down dough and turn out onto a floured surface. Knead in sugar cubes and cinnamon into dough, being careful to not overmix. Flatten dough into a rectangle about 10 inches long, with the short end being the same length as your bread pan (about 8½ inches). Then roll it up, pushing in protruding chunks of sugar, and place it in the pan, seam side down.

Cover and let rise for about 30 more minutes. Preheat the oven to 350 degrees. Brush top of loaf with oil and sprinkle on sugar and bake for 30 to 35 minutes, until it is golden brown and sounds hollow when tapped with a spoon. Remove from bread pan and let cool on cooling rack. Store leftover bread covered at room temperature.

Yield: 10 SLICES

Prep time: 35 MINUTES ACTIVE

Difficulty:

DESSERT PIZZA

When I was in college, I ate my share of truly nasty dessert pizza from a major pizza chain. Once I started making my own pizza, I wanted a sweet, but not greasy, treat. Drizzled with icing, this dessert pizza is worth saving room for.

DOUGH:

1 packet (¼ ounce or 2¼ teaspoons) active dry yeast

1 teaspoon sugar

½ cup warm water

1 cup flour

½ teaspoon salt

1 tablespoon oil

¼ cup raisins

TOPPING:

¼ cup sugar

1 tablespoon cinnamon

2 tablespoons margarine, melted

½ recipe White Icing (page 155)

For Dough: In a small bowl, combine yeast, sugar and water. Let sit for about 5 minutes, or until foamy. In a large bowl, combine flour and salt. Add yeast mixture, oil and raisins. Mix until a soft dough comes together. Turn out onto a floured surface and knead for about 4 to 5 minutes or until dough is smooth and elastic. Place in an oiled bowl and turn to coat. Cover with a kitchen towel and let rise in a warm place for 40 minutes or until doubled in size.

Preheat the oven to 450 degrees if baking pizza on a pizza pan, or 500 degrees if baking on a pizza stone. Turn dough out onto a lightly floured surface. Roll out with a rolling pin or push with your hands to create a 10-inch disc. If using a pizza pan, bake for 7 to 10 minutes, or until golden. If using a pizza stone, bake for about 5 minutes or until golden.

For Topping: Combine cinnamon and sugar in a small bowl.

Remove pizza from the oven and brush each side with melted butter. Sprinkle with cinnamon sugar mixture and drizzle with a half batch of White Icing. Cut into slices with a pizza cutter. Store leftover pizza covered in fridge.

Yield: 1 PIZZA, 6 SLICES
Prep time: 25 MINUTES ACTIVE
Difficulty:

KIDS IN THE KITCHEN

When I was a child, baking seemed like the most magical thing on Earth. The ingredients were sacred and reserved for holidays and special occasions. I had my own special set of child-sized kitchenware and could frequently be found forcing my mother or grandparents to eat my latest inedible creation. Luckily for you, the recipes here are very delicious, so you won't have any problems chowing down on these treats.

While these recipes are meant to be made by and with kids (but not just for kids), it's important to gauge your own child's abilities. Trade places and be their kitchen helper to ensure that their masterpieces are safely crafted to perfection.

Vegan-Bake Oven Treats

When I was about four or five, I received an Easy-Bake Oven for Christmas. It is one of the most exciting memories from my childhood. Whenever you have anything your size as a child, it's quite a treat, but this actually produced things that tasted good, too! My little mind was blown. It was more exciting than *An American Tail*, Madonna and My Little Pony combined. A few years ago, as a childless adult who owns a house and has her own big-girl oven, I decided to buy an Easy-Bake Oven to make mini treats again and to do some experimenting. Those little prepackaged mixes the Easy-Bake comes with are not vegan, and their laundry list of ingredients isn't something I would want my kids to eat, so the quest to create quick and vegan Easy-Bake recipes began.

The bonus to this is that due to a, um, faulty oven, I had to figure out how to continue baking with my little pans when the Easy-Bake stopped working. Luckily, these recipes easily adapt to a toaster oven, so if you have some little pans around, you can easily whip up these treats in a toaster oven. You can look for small pans at regular stores where they sell things like mini Bundt-cake pans. Because these recipes are so quick, they are best eaten immediately; Vegan-Bake Oven treats do not have the same shelf life as regular baked goods.

My disclaimer, to state the obvious, is that your child should never bake unattended, even with an Easy–Bake Oven or toaster oven; they can be just as dangerous as a regular oven. The cake recipes use a standard Easy-Bake cake pan, and the cookies can be baked on the appropriate Easy-Bake pan or on a toaster pan in your toaster oven.

On to the lil' grub!

- LIL' YELLOW CAKE
- LIL' CHOCOLATE CAKE
- LIL' CAKE TOPPINGS
- LIL' CHOCOLATE CHIPPERS
- LIL' PEANUT BUTTER DROPS
- LIL' THUMBPRINTS
- ICE CREAM SAMMIES
- OOPLE AND BANOONOO JAR BREAD
- OATEY NUTTER BUTTER BARS
- DRIZZLED CINN-A-SCONES
- WHOLE WORLD IN MY HANDS CUPCAKES
- BEST CUT-OUT SUGAR COOKIES

LiL' Yellow Cake

Aptly named the Lil' Cake by my husband, Jim, this small cake is perfect for a tea party or after-school snack. You can top it with a little icing or some melted chocolate chips, or you can add sprinkles or just a spoonful of jam. It's always nice to share, so cut off a piece for a friend or bake up a second one to share with your kitchen helper.

5 teaspoons flour
1 tablespoon sugar
¼ teaspoon baking powder
¼ teaspoon oil
5 teaspoons milk

Preheat the Easy-Bake Oven by turning it on, or preheat the toaster oven to 375 degrees. Lightly grease and flour a single little cake pan.

In a small bowl, combine flour, sugar and baking powder. Add oil and milk and whisk with a fork. Pour batter into the prepared pan. Bake for 13 to 15 minutes, until cake is slightly golden and a toothpick comes out clean. Let cake cool completely, then run a butter knife around the edge and invert to remove cake from pan. Top with the topping of your choice.

Yield: 1 LIL' CAKE
Prep time: 5 MINUTES
Difficulty:

Lil' Chocolate Cake

Chocolate cake and yellow cake, yin and yang. This cake is especially good with jam on top. If you have two pans, you can make one batch of chocolate batter and one yellow and then put half in each pan and swirl them together. Yummy!

4 teaspoons flour
1 teaspoon baking cocoa
1 tablespoon sugar
¼ teaspoon baking soda
¼ teaspoon oil
4 teaspoons milk

Preheat the Easy-Bake Oven by turning it on, or preheat the toaster oven to 375 degrees. Lightly grease and flour a single little cake pan.

In a small bowl, combine flour, cocoa, sugar and baking soda. Add oil and milk and whisk with a fork until combined. Pour batter into the prepared pan and bake for 13 to 15 minutes, until center is set and a toothpick comes out clean. Let cake cool completely, then run a butter knife around the edge and invert to remove cake from pan. Top with the topping of your choice.

Yield: 1 LIL' CAKE
Prep time: 3 MINUTES
Difficulty:

Lil' Cake Toppings

Chocolate Topping: Melt 2 teaspoons chocolate chips in the microwave in 7-second intervals, stirring between each one, until smooth and creamy. Spread on top of cake.

Icing: Stir ¼ teaspoon milk into 3 tablespoons powdered sugar. Drizzle on top of cake.

Fruit: Spread 1 tablespoon jam on top of cake.

Prep time: 5 MINUTES
Difficulty:

Lil' Chocolate Chippers

Little bite-sized chocolate chip cookies are the best, especially when you make them yourself! A grown-up kitchen helper should chop up the chocolate chips into small pieces.

3 tablespoons sugar

1½ teaspoons margarine, melted

5 tablespoons plus 1 teaspoon flour

1 teaspoon milk

1 tablespoon chocolate chips, chopped

Preheat the Easy-Bake Oven by turning it on, or preheat the toaster oven to 375 degrees.

In a small bowl, mix sugar and margarine with a fork. Add flour and combine until crumbly, then add milk and stir to make dough soft and smooth. Stir in chocolate chips. Spoon ½ teaspoon-sized cookies onto a little baking sheet or use a little cake pan, leaving a ½ inch between each cookie. Bake for 5 minutes and let cool for 10 minutes before eating.

Yield: 1 DOZEN LIL' COOKIES

Prep time: 10 MINUTES

Difficulty:

Lil' Peanut Butter Drops

These cookies can be made with any nut butter you like, not just peanut butter. The cookies get rolled in some sugar for a crunchy coating, and after baking, each cookie gets topped with a little chocolate chip drop—the perfect finishing touch!

1 teaspoon oil

1 tablespoon peanut butter

1 tablespoon plus 1 teaspoon sugar

3 tablespoons flour

1½ teaspoons milk

2 teaspoons sugar, for rolling

12 chocolate chips

Preheat the Easy-Bake Oven by turning it on, or preheat the toaster oven to 375 degrees.

In a small bowl, combine oil and peanut butter. Add sugar and mix well. Add flour until crumbly and then stir in milk. Spoon out ½ teaspoon-sized cookies and roll in the remaining 2 teaspoons of sugar. Slightly flatten each cookie. Place cookies on a little baking sheet or use a little cake pan, leaving ½ inch between each cookie. Bake for 5 minutes. Remove cookies from the oven and place one chocolate chip on top of each cookie, lightly pressing down. Let cool for 10 minutes before eating.

Yield: 1 DOZEN LIL' COOKIES

Prep time: 10 MINUTES

Difficulty:

LIL' THUMBPRINTS

These cookies are delicious. It's fun to poke your thumb (or pointer finger or pinkie!) into the dough, and it's even more fun to eat! Buttery cookies with a little thumbprint filled with jam make a yummy treat.

1 tablespoon margarine, melted
1 tablespoon sugar
3 tablespoons flour
½ teaspoon milk
2 teaspoons jam

Preheat the Easy-Bake Oven by turning it on, or preheat the toaster oven to 375 degrees.

In a small bowl, combine margarine and sugar. Add flour and milk and stir together to make a soft dough. Roll dough into ½ teaspoon-sized balls. Place on a little baking sheet or a little cake pan about ½ inch apart and make a small thumbprint indent in the middle of each cookie. Bake for 5 minutes. Let cool for 10 minutes and then spoon a little bit of jam into the thumbprint of each cookie.

Yield: 1 DOZEN LIL' COOKIES
Prep time: 10 MINUTES
Difficulty:

ICE CREAM SAMMIES

These ice cream sammie cookies are chewy and chocolatey, just like a good ice cream sammie should be! Use your favorite cookie cutters to cut out fun-shaped sammies. (I'm sure you'll have no problems eating up the cookie scraps.)

⅓ cup margarine, softened
⅔ cup sugar
2 tablespoons applesauce
½ teaspoon vanilla
¾ cup flour
⅓ cup baking cocoa, sifted
½ teaspoon baking powder
⅛ teaspoon salt

Preheat the oven to 375 degrees. Line a baking sheet with parchment paper.

In a medium bowl, combine margarine and sugar. Add applesauce and vanilla and mix well. In a small bowl, combine flour, cocoa, baking powder and salt. Add dry ingredients to wet ingredients and mix thoroughly. Turn dough out onto the prepared baking sheet. Place a sheet of waxed paper over dough and roll out into a square about ¼-inch thick. Remove waxed paper and bake dough for 10 to 12 minutes. Remove from oven and let cool for about 15 minutes.

Use cookie cutters to cut out shapes for the ice cream sammies while the cookie square is still warm. Make sure to cut 2 identical shapes at a time so each sammie has a top and bottom. Remove shapes and let them completely cool on a cooling rack. Take ice cream out of the freezer to let it soften for about 20 minutes. Scoop out ice cream onto one cookie and press a matching cookie on top to smoosh the ice cream down. Wrap each sammie in plastic wrap and put in the freezer to set, at least 20 minutes. Store sammies wrapped in plastic wrap in the freezer.

Yield: ABOUT 8 SAMMIES
Prep time: 10 MINUTES
Difficulty: 🥄

OOPPLE AND BANOONOO JAR BREAD

I just love the "Apples and Bananas" song, and I know you will love this bread. The combination of apples and bananas smells amazing and creates a delicious, moist bread. You can top it with sugar, as suggested below, or a sprinkling of nuts, such as walnuts or pecans. This bread is baked in mason jars and is a delicious and fun bread to give as gifts to teachers or friends.

2 cups flour

1 teaspoon baking soda

½ teaspoon baking powder

¼ teaspoon salt

½ teaspoon cinnamon

½ cup oil

1 cup sugar

⅓ cup milk

1 teaspoon vinegar

1 cup mashed bananas
(about 2 large or 3 small bananas)

2 medium tart apples,
peeled and shredded

Preheat the oven to 375 degrees. Lightly grease the insides of 6 half-pint (8-ounce) mason jars.

In a medium bowl, combine flour, baking soda, baking powder, salt and cinnamon. In a large bowl, combine oil and sugar. Add milk and vinegar and mix well. Stir in bananas and apples. Add dry ingredients to wet ingredients in batches, until just mixed. If you want to be able to put lids on the jars, fill them ⅔ full with batter. If you want a little bit of bread to stick out of the top of the jars, fill them ¾ full.

Sprinkle a little extra sugar on top of batter in each jar. Place jars on a baking sheet and bake for 20 to 25 minutes or until tops are browned and a toothpick comes out clean. Let bread cool completely on a cooling rack. Store bread covered at room temperature.

Yield: 6 HALF-PINT LOAVES
Prep time: 30 MINUTES
Difficulty:

OATEY NUTTER-BUTTER BARS

These bars are delicious! They are nutty, chewy and full of tasty things like oats, peanut butter and raisins and are perfect for an after-school snack. You can always substitute a different nut butter, so play around with almond, cashew or even sunflower-seed butter.

1 cup flour
½ cup quick oats
1 teaspoon baking powder
1 teaspoon baking soda
⅛ teaspoon salt
¼ cup oil
⅔ cup sugar
⅓ cup applesauce
½ cup peanut butter
⅓ cup raisins
⅓ cup chocolate chips

Preheat the oven to 350 degrees. Line an 8 x 8-inch baking pan with parchment paper or lightly grease it with oil or margarine.

In a large bowl, mix together flour, oats, baking powder, baking soda and salt. In a medium bowl, combine oil and sugar and mix until well-combined. Stir in applesauce and mix until well-combined (you may need to use a whisk or an electric hand mixer on low speed). Add wet ingredients to dry ingredients and mix well, making sure to scrape the bottom of the bowl for pockets of flour. Stir in raisins and chocolate chips.

Spread batter onto prepared baking sheet and bake for 38 to 42 minutes, until bars are lightly browned on the edges and set in the middle. Let bars cool in the pan on a cooling rack for at least 45 minutes before cutting. Store bars covered at room temperature.

Yield: 16 BARS
Prep time: 20 MINUTES
Difficulty:

DRIZZLED CINN-A-SCONES

These scones are a mixture of snickerdoodles and biscuits. It's fun to cut them out and then roll them in the cinnamon sugar and even more fun to drizzle the icing in zig-zags or swirls.

1 cup flour
1 teaspoon baking soda
¼ cup plus 1 tablespoon sugar
⅛ teaspoon salt
2 tablespoons cold margarine
⅓ cup milk
½ teaspoon mild vinegar
1 teaspoon cinnamon
1 recipe White Icing (page 155)

Preheat the oven to 425 degrees. Line a baking sheet with parchment paper.

In a medium bowl, combine flour, baking soda, 1 tablespoon sugar and salt. Mix in margarine with the back of a fork until it is broken up and crumbly. In a separate small bowl, combine milk and vinegar and let sit for a minute. Combine milk with dry ingredients and mix until just combined (the mixture might be a little dry).

Combine remaining ¼ cup sugar and cinnamon in a small bowl. Sprinkle half of sugar mixture on a clean, dry surface and set the rest aside. Gently roll out the scone dough onto the sugared surface until it's about 1 inch thick. Cut out scones using a juice glass or small biscuit cutter. Roll each biscuit in reserved sugar mixture to coat and place on the baking sheet.

Bake for 10 minutes, until scones have risen and are lightly golden. Let scones cool completely and then drizzle zig-zags on top with White Icing. Store scones covered at room temperature.

Yield: 6 SCONES
Prep time: 15 MINUTES
Difficulty: 🥢

WHOLE WORLD IN MY HANDS CUPCAKES

These cupcakes are delicious and fun! Because half of the batter is blue and half of it is green, they look like miniature planet Earths in the palm of your hand. They would be fun to make for Earth Day or just because they taste great! Eat through the continents and the oceans down the chocolate center of the Earth. You can even place a red candy in the bottom of each cupcake liner to make the red-hot core.

BASE:

12 chocolate sandwich cookies, crushed

¼ cup flour

2 tablespoons baking cocoa

¼ cup milk

¼ cup chocolate chips

. . . .

Bake the batter in a 9-inch cake pan for an extra 15 to 20 minutes and serve with Blueberries & Cream Sauce (page 160) to make a We are the World Cake!

EARTH:

1 cup plus 2 tablespoons flour

1 teaspoon baking soda

½ teaspoon baking powder

⅛ teaspoon salt

½ cup sugar

¼ cup oil

1 cup milk

1 teaspoon vinegar

½ teaspoon vanilla

blue and green food coloring

. . . .

If you want a topping, brush on a thin layer of "clouds" by combining 1 teaspoon of milk with ½ cup of powdered sugar. The mixture should be thin enough to brush on, so you can still see the Earth underneath.

Preheat the oven to 350 degrees. Line a muffin tin with 12 cupcake liners.

For Base: In a small bowl, combine crushed sandwich cookies, flour and cocoa. Stir in milk and chocolate chips. Evenly spoon the chocolate mixture into the bottom of each cupcake liner.

For Earth: In a small bowl, combine flour, baking soda, baking powder and salt. In a large bowl, combine sugar and oil. Stir in milk and vinegar, then stir in vanilla. Using an electric hand mixer, add dry ingredients to wet ingredients in two batches and mix until well-incorporated. Divide batter between two bowls. In one bowl, add several drops of blue food coloring and in the other bowl add several drops of green food coloring until the color is very vivid (it will fade slightly when baked). Mix each bowl well. Drop alternating spoonfuls of batter into each cupcake liner, filling the liners ¾ full. Swirl the colors using a toothpick. Bake for 15 to 20 minutes or until a toothpick comes out clean. Let cool in the muffin tin for 15 minutes, then transfer to a rack to finish cooling. Store cupcakes covered at room temperature.

Yield: 12 CUPCAKES
Prep time: 25 MINUTES
Difficulty:

BEST CUT-OUT SUGAR COOKIES

These classic cut-out sugar cookies are the vegan version of the cookies my grandmother made every year for Christmas! Bust out your favorite cookie cutters and cut away to make these sweet, crisp treats. Decorate with icing and sprinkles and then share your hard work with friends.

1½ cups flour

½ teaspoon baking powder

½ cup margarine, softened

½ cup sugar

3 tablespoons applesauce

1 tablespoon milk

½ teaspoon vanilla

White Icing Recipe (page 155)

Food coloring and sprinkles (optional)

In a small bowl, combine flour and baking powder. In a large bowl, cream together margarine and sugar. Add applesauce, milk and vanilla and mix to combine. Add dry ingredients in batches until a soft dough forms. Wrap dough in plastic wrap and chill in the fridge for at least 30 minutes, or as long as overnight.

Preheat the oven to 350 degrees. Line two baking sheets with parchment paper.

On a clean, floured surface, roll out dough to about ¼-inch thick. Cut out shapes with cookie cutters and place on baking sheets. Bake for 10 to 12 minutes, until cookies have puffed up a bit. Rotate baking sheets halfway through if baking more than one sheet at a time. If you want soft cookies, remove them from oven before they turn golden (about 9 to 10 minutes). If you prefer them a little crisper, bake until they are lightly golden on the edges. Remove from the oven and let cool on a rack for 10 minutes, then transfer cookies directly to the rack to cool completely.

If you're using food coloring, mix up one batch of White Icing for each color you want to ice with or mix up a double batch of plain White Icing. Apply icing to cookies with a butter knife. Add any sprinkles while icing is still wet. Store cookies covered at room temperature.

Yield: ABOUT 2 DOZEN COOKIES

Prep time: 15 MINUTES ACTIVE

Difficulty: 🥄

Frostings, Icings & Toppings

Frostings, icings, toppings and sauces are the finishing touches that take something good and make it great. This chapter is full of delicious treats to dress up your favorite baked goods, and there are a lot of possibilities for mixing and matching different toppings and baked goods to create new treats.

- WHITE ICING
- CREAM CHEESE FROSTING
- PEANUT BUTTER FROSTING
- CHOCOLATE FROSTING
- FUDGY FROSTING
- BUTTERCREAM FROSTING
- LEMON FROSTING
- COCONUT GLAZE
- PEPPERMINT ICING
- CHOCOLATE GANACHE
- BLUEBERRIES & CREAM SAUCE

White Icing

You have probably noticed that I use this icing often. It is truly the finishing touch on many different items and can transform a good baked good into something sublime.

2 tablespoons milk

1½ to 2 cups powdered sugar, sifted

In a small bowl, whisk milk and powdered sugar together to desired thickness. If icing is thinner, it will drizzle easily, but you can always scoop it into a plastic bag and snip off a tiny bit of a corner to apply the icing more precisely to your baked goods. A little liquid goes a long way, so add just a few extra drops of milk to thin it out to a glaze consistency.

Yield: ⅓ CUP
Prep time: 5 MINUTES
Difficulty: 🥄

Cream Cheese Frosting

This recipe is wonderful on Forever Carrot Cake (page 86), but feel free to try it on other things too. This makes enough to frost the tops and sides of a 9-inch layered cake.

1 8-ounce container soy cream cheese, room temperature

¼ cup margarine, softened

1 teaspoon vanilla

2 to 2½ cups sifted powdered sugar

In a large bowl with an electric hand mixer, cream together cream cheese, margarine and vanilla on medium speed. Add powdered sugar and blend to desired taste and thickness (more sugar = stiffer frosting).

Yield: 2 CUPS
Prep time: 10 MINUTES
Difficulty: 🥄

PEANUT BUTTER FROSTING

This frosting is just peanut buttery enough to please nut fans, but it's still very creamy and light. Try it with other nut butters if you can't eat peanuts—almond butter would be lovely. This recipe will frost the tops and sides of a 9-inch double-layer cake.

1 8-ounce container soy cream cheese, room temperature

2 tablespoons margarine, softened

¼ cup peanut butter (or more, to taste)

2 to 2½ cups sifted powdered sugar

In a large bowl, beat cream cheese, margarine and peanut butter with an electric hand mixer. Add powdered sugar and blend to desired taste and consistency. Add more sugar or nut butter to taste.

Yield: 2 CUPS
Prep time: 10 MINUTES
Difficulty: 🥄🥄

. . . .

The key to this frosting is subtlety of the peanut butter. If you add too much peanut butter, the frosting will become oily, so be sure to taste-test after any additional scoops.

CHOCOLATE FROSTING

This is a great, all-purpose chocolate frosting. It is perfect for decorating cakes with an icing bag, or you can just slather it on there and enjoy! This recipe will frost the tops and sides of a 9-inch double-layer cake.

2 ounces bitter- or semisweet chocolate

½ cup margarine, softened

1 teaspoon vanilla

2½ to 3 cups powdered sugar, sifted

2 tablespoons milk

In a glass bowl over a pot filled with water, or very carefully and slowly in the microwave, melt the chocolate. Let sit to cool slightly. In a large bowl, with an electric hand mixer on low speed, cream together chocolate and margarine. Mix in vanilla and powdered sugar until mixture is a little crumbly. Add just enough milk to make frosting smooth to desired consistency.

Yield: 1½ CUPS
Prep time: 15 MINUTES
Difficulty: 🥄🥄

FUDGY FROSTING

When I went to college, I bought containers of fudge frosting and ate spoonfuls of it as a treat. And I wondered how I gained my freshman fifteen! This fudge frosting is thick and creamy and reminds me of those indulgent days of skipping class and watching reruns of Saved by the Bell *with a spoon of frosting in my mouth. This recipe will frost the top and sides of a 9-inch single-layer cake or a pan of bars.*

⅓ cup chocolate chips

3 tablespoons margarine

1 cup powdered sugar, sifted

pinch of salt

3 tablespoons milk

¼ teaspoon vanilla

In a saucepan, combine chocolate chips and margarine and heat over medium heat until melted, stirring continuously. Pour out mixture into a medium bowl and whisk in powdered sugar, salt, milk and vanilla until combined. Let frosting set in the fridge for 15 minutes before using.

Yield: 1 CUP
Prep time: 10 MINUTES
Difficulty:

BUTTERCREAM FROSTING

Simple, classic buttercream. This is a go-to frosting when you want something light and creamy to dress up your dessert. This recipe will frost 12 cupcakes or a 9-inch single-layer cake.

3 tablespoons margarine, room temperature

1 tablespoon shortening, room temperature

¼ teaspoon vanilla

2 to 2½ cups powdered sugar, sifted

2 to 3 tablespoons milk

In a large bowl, cream margarine and shortening with an electric hand mixer until well blended. Add vanilla. Add powdered sugar, ½ cup at a time, until mixture is crumbly. Incorporate milk 1 tablespoon at a time until mixture is fluffy and spreadable. Adjust milk and powdered sugar until frosting is at desired consistency.

Yield: 1 CUP
Prep time: 10 MINUTES
Difficulty:

LEMON FROSTING

This Lemon Frosting is the perfect blend of sweet creaminess and tart lemon. While it's obviously a great frosting, it is also delicious as a dip with your favorite fresh-cut fruit. This recipe will frost a pan of bars or a 9-inch single-layer cake.

½ of an 8-ounce container soy cream cheese

1 tablespoon margarine, room temperature

½ teaspoon lemon zest

2 teaspoons lemon juice

2½ to 3 cups powdered sugar, sifted

Using an electric hand mixer, cream together cream cheese and margarine. Add lemon juice and zest. Blend in powdered sugar 1 cup at a time until frosting reaches desired thickness.

Yield: 1¼ CUPS
Prep time: 10 MINUTES
Difficulty: 🥄

COCONUT GLAZE

This glaze is super on Tropical Coconut Cake (page 95), but it can also be used for lots of other treats. Thicken it up a little and try it on Baked Chocolate-Glazed Donuts (page 126) for a change of pace!

2 tablespoons low-fat coconut milk

2 tablespoons milk

1½ to 2 cups powdered sugar, sifted

In a small bowl, whisk together coconut milk and powdered sugar until glaze reaches desired consistency. Pour over cooled cake.

Yield: ½ CUP
Prep time: 5 MINUTES
Difficulty: 🥄

PEPPERMINT ICING

This icing is like a Peppermint Patty sans chocolate. The peppermint flavor is distinct and creamy but never overpowers.

4 teaspoons milk

¼ teaspoon peppermint extract

1½ cups powdered sugar, sifted

In a small bowl combine milk, peppermint extract and powdered sugar and stir until smooth. Depending on how you prefer your icing, you may want it thicker, like a glaze, or thinner, like a spreadable icing. Add small splashes of milk to thin the icing or add additional powdered sugar 2 tablespoons at a time to thicken it to desired consistency.

Yield: ½ CUP

Prep time: 5 MINUTES

Difficulty: 🥄

CHOCOLATE GANACHE

This ganache is perfect to top off a creamy Boston Cream Pie (page 91) but is also great for dipping fruit in. It can be refrigerated to help it set, but it will harden if it is left in there for a while. If you store your leftover cake in the fridge, be sure to let it sit out at room temperature for a few minutes to let the ganache soften before serving.

¼ cup margarine

3 tablespoons milk, room temperature

½ cup chocolate chips

In a small sauce pan over medium-low heat, melt margarine completely, stirring constantly. Add milk and whisk to combine. Remove from heat and add chocolate chips, stirring rapidly to melt. Let ganache cool completely to room temperature, stirring from time to time to keep a crust from developing, then spread cooled ganache over the top of the cake.

Yield: ¾ CUP

Prep time: 15 MINUTES ACTIVE

Difficulty: 🥄🥄

BLUEBERRIES & CREAM SAUCE

This creamy sauce is soooooo good! I can hardly keep from spooning it straight from the pot and into my mouth. The higher the fat content of your sauce, the thicker it will be, so I recommend using soy milk, but I've also used almond milk and rice milk and the sauce has been delicious every time.

½ cup sugar

1 tablespoon plus 1 teaspoon cornstarch

1 cup milk

½ teaspoon good quality vanilla

½ cup fresh blueberries, or ½ cup frozen blueberries, thawed and drained

In a small saucepan, whisk together sugar and cornstarch until well-combined. Whisk in milk and cook over medium-high heat until mixture reaches a boil, whisking continuously. Lower heat to a simmer, stirring constantly, until sauce thickens enough to coat the back of a spoon, about 5 to 7 minutes. Add vanilla and let simmer for one more minute. Remove from heat and pour sauce into a bowl. Let chill in the fridge or freezer for 10 to 15 minutes or until it is a bit more set but is still warm. Add blueberries and gently stir to combine. Do not overmix blueberries or sauce will look blueish-gray. Serve warm or cold over Blackest Forest Cake (page 94) or on top of just about any treat your heart desires.

Yield: 1½ CUPS
Prep time: 15 MINUTES ACTIVE
Difficulty:

RECIPE INDEX

OTHER ULYSSES PRESS BOOKS

Have Your Cake and Vegan Too: 50 Dazzling and Delicious Cake Creations

Kris Holechek, $16.95

Featuring color photos, this book offers everything from quick and easy coffee cakes to layered birthday extravaganzas. Smashing the stereotypes of vegan baking, *Have Your Cake and Vegan Too* has easy-to-follow directions that show readers the tricks for vegan-baking success.

The 100 Best Gluten-Free Recipes for Your Vegan Kitchen: Delicious Smoothies, Soups, Salads, Entrees, and Desserts

Kelly E. Keough, $14.95

Being vegan is a culinary challenge, especially when you are avoiding gluten. This book shows how to address both restrictions without sacrificing flavor or adding hours in the kitchen. These mouth-watering recipes draw on the best natural animal and wheat substitutes to create savory and sweet favorites

The I Love Trader Joe's Cookbook: Over 150 Delicious Recipes Using Only Foods from the World's Greatest Grocery Store

Cherie Mercer Twohy, $17.95

Based on the author's wildly popular, standing-room-only workshops, *The I Love Trader Joe's Cookbook* presents her top recipes for everything from crowd-pleasing hors d'oeuvres and tasty quick meals to gourmet entrées and world-class desserts.

The Juice Fasting Bible: Discover the Power of an All-Juice Diet to Restore Good Health, Lose Weight and Increase Vitality

Dr. Sandra Cabot, $12.95

Offering a series of quick and easy juice fasts, this book provides a reader-friendly approach to an increasingly popular alternative health practice.

Raw Juicing: The Healthy, Easy and Delicious Way to Gain the Benefits of the Raw Food Lifestyle

Leslie Kenton, $12.95

As the health benefits of eating uncooked food become widely acknowledged, more people are looking for ways to "go raw." This book's raw-juice plan and great-tasting recipes offer the easiest way to "go raw" for a meal: Make a super-healthy, delicious raw juice drink.

Sugar-Free Gluten-Free Baking and Desserts: Recipes for Healthy and Delicious Cookies, Cakes, Muffins, Scones, Pies, Puddings, Breads and Pizzas

Kelly Keough, $14.95

Shows readers how to bring taboo treats back to the baking sheet with savory recipes that swap wheat for wholesome alternatives like quinoa, arrowroot and tapioca starch, and trade in sugar for natural sweeteners like agave, yacon and stevia.

To order these books call 800-377-2542 or 510-601-8301, fax 510-601-8307, e-mail ulysses@ulyssespress.com, or write to Ulysses Press, P.O. Box 3440, Berkeley, CA 94703. All retail orders are shipped free of charge. California residents must include sales tax. Allow two to three weeks for delivery.

About the Author

Kris Holechek is a vegan master baker, cookbook author and blogger. She is the author of *Have Your Cake and Vegan Too: 50 Dazzling and Delicious Cake Creations* and *The Damn Tasty! Vegan Baking Guide*, and the writer of nomnomnomblog.com. Kris lives in Eugene, Oregon, where she geeks out on food science and linguistics with her husband and three cats.